THE MODERN JAPANESE PRINT

BOOKS BY JAMES A. MICHENER

THE MODERN JAPANESE PRINT: An Appreciation

THE HOKUSAI SKETCHBOOKS: Selections from the Manga

JAPANESE PRINTS: From the Early Masters to the Modern

SAYONARA

THE BRIDGE AT ANDAU

with A. Grove Day
RASCALS IN PARADISE

THE FIRES OF SPRING

HAWAII

THE BRIDGES AT TOKO-RI

TALES OF THE SOUTH PACIFIC

CARAVANS

THE SOURCE

RETURN TO PARADISE

THE VOICE OF ASIA

THE FLOATING WORLD

JAMES A. MICHENER

THE MODERN JAPANESE PRINT
AN APPRECIATION

with ten prints by
HIRATSUKA UN'ICHI · MAEKAWA SEMPAN
MORI YOSHITOSHI · WATANABE SADAO · KINOSHITA TOMIO
SHIMA TAMAMI · AZECHI UMETARO · IWAMI REIKA
YOSHIDA MASAJI · MAKI HAKU

CHARLES E. TUTTLE COMPANY: PUBLISHERS
Rutland, Vermont & Tokyo, Japan

Representatives
Continental Europe: BOXERBOOKS, INC., *Zurich*
British Isles: PRENTICE-HALL INTERNATIONAL, INC., *London*
Australasia: PAUL FLESCH & CO., PTY. LTD., *Melbourne*
Canada: M. G. HURTIG LTD., *Edmonton*

Published by the Charles E. Tuttle Company, Inc.
of Rutland, Vermont & Tokyo, Japan
with editorial offices at
Suido 1-chome, 2-6, Bunkyo-ku, Tokyo, Japan

Copyright in Japan, 1968, by Charles E. Tuttle Co., Inc.

Library of Congress Catalog Card No. 62–17555

First popular edition, 1968

PRINTED IN JAPAN

TABLE OF CONTENTS

5

PUBLISHER'S FOREWORD

IN 1959 James Michener came to us with a unique and challenging idea. He wanted us to publish, in a deluxe format, an edition of original contemporary Japanese woodblock prints. Mr. Michener's reasons for making this request derived from his personal interest in the woodblock artists of Japan and, as he saw it then, their almost insurmountable struggle to make a living from their art.

As publishers devoted to the concept of cultural interchange between the East and West, we quickly caught Mr. Michener's enthusiasm and agreed to the project.

Then the work began. How should we determine which of the hundreds and thousands of contemporary woodblock prints might be included? We decided to sponsor a contest to be judged by a panel of qualified art experts in the United States and Japan. From a total of 275 prints submitted by 120 artists, ten were chosen as best representing "the richness and power of the modern Japanese print movement." The final selection is a beautiful and significant set of prints, running the stylistic gamut from representational to abstract, from typically Japanese to international, including both great old names and newcomers who are sure to become great.

Finally, in 1962, *The Modern Japanese Print—An Appreciation* appeared as a limited edition of 475 copies in imperial folio size. The paper was the finest of handmade Japanese vellum; the binding, three colors of pure, fine-weave hemp cloth. It is a book in which we, and the author, take considerable pride, for it is more than a book; it is a work of art.

The Modern Japanese Print met with wide critical and commercial acclaim. Now, several years later, it has been suggested that we bring out a popularly priced edition, thus displaying to a far wider audience the techniques and craftsmanship of this group of distinguished artists, along with Mr. Michener's perceptive, informative commentary.

James Michener heartily endorses this version of what originated as a collector's item. We present this volume with renewed pride.

INTRODUCTION

IN the early summer of 1959, business required that I be in Tokyo during an exciting time in my life: word kept trickling through from New York telling of the unexpected good things that were happening to a novel I had recently completed, and it looked as if it might be a success. For five years I had worked on the novel, and to have it accepted was encouraging, but the degree of success promised by these first reports went well beyond my expectation. Thus early in the life of the book I was assured that the time I had invested in its writing would be repaid; whether or not the public would like the book would be determined later.

As a result of the good news, I found myself assured of financial independence for a few more years, and I began to reflect upon how unfairly modern society distributes the rewards of art. I knew literally hundreds of able writers who found it impossible to earn a living, while to a few all good things happened. Once I myself had labored at writing for eight years without being able to earn a nickel, and I had been as good a writer then as I was now. Those who try to be artists exist in a world of nothing or everything, and I wish it were not so.

It was in this mood that I was drifting down Tokyo's Ginza one sunny afternoon, idly watching the flow of life along that enchanting thoroughfare. With nothing better to do, I turned west and passed into the warren of little streets and alleys known as the Nishi Ginza. Soon I found myself standing before a window I had grown to know; it belonged to the print shop and art gallery called Yoseido, opened in 1954 by Abè Yuji, third-generation representative of a family of art-mounters which had formerly been appointed to mount scrolls, screens, and the like for the Imperial Household and had also become prosperous in Ginza real estate. Ever since Yoseido's opening, the artistically-minded young Abè had served as the principal salesman for a group of artists who had made something of a splash in the art world.

I entered Yoseido that afternoon and saw on its walls the latest prints by artists I had come to know well. Here was a brilliantly colored alpine scene by Azechi Umetaro, and I studied the manner in which this delightful mountaineer had progressed to new understandings of his art. On the other wall was a marvelous, somber abstraction by Yoshida Masaji, a brooding thing of gray and black and purple, and again I lost myself in contemplating the various plateaus of progress across which this young man had moved in the years I had known him.

Also prominent was a large print in stark black and white, an architectural scene carved in the most ancient tradition by the oldest of the artists, little Hiratsuka Un'ichi, who had been my close friend for many years and who was still one of the greatest of contemporary woodblock artists, regardless of what country one was considering.

Here before me was the work which fifty men had accomplished in the two years since I had last met with them: the scintillating color prints, the vibrant black-and-whites, those done in the old style, and those so modern that they clawed at the mind for recognition. It was a body of magnificent work, one group's summary of how men saw the world and its passions.

As I looked at the prints I could see behind each one the man who had carved those blocks and pressed that paper down into the splashed colors. They were as fine a group of men as I have ever known: schoolteachers, mechanics, intellectual hermits, wild, gusty men who loved to drink, mountaineers, factory workers, poets of the most exquisite sensibility, laughing men, sober men, tragic men. And as I saw their faces staring back at me I experienced a real sickness of the soul, and out of that sickness came this book.

For I, by pure accident, worked in a field (writing) in a society (America) that assured me a decent income, a good living, and some security for the future. But those men on the wall, most of them with a far greater talent than mine, were laboring in a field (print-making) in a country (Japan) that provided only the most meager living, if any. Of all the woodblock artists I have known in Japan only two have been able to make a living from their art, and they have worked like dogs to accomplish even this. All the others have had to devote their principal energies to irrelevant jobs.

It has always seemed to me most unfair that a world which, whether it acknowledges the fact or not, requires art just as much as it requires rice has never discovered a way in which to reward the artist sensibly. A young American, talented to be sure, writes a book about a man who wears gray-flannel suits and from it earns more than a million dollars. Another young American whose equal talents run to poetry cannot even begin to make a living. A third young American with more talent than either of his compatriots turns to sculpturing and literally starves.

Or, to take a specific example, I spend five years at a major project and before it is even published I am assured security for two or three years, while Yoshida Masaji, in Tokyo, works for the same length of time on his statement of a major theme and from it gains almost nothing. Tormented by these injustices, I decided that the least I could do would be to purchase still more of the work of my friends; so I quickly bought all of their recent prints and lugged them back to my hotel room. There, with the help of a maid and a box of thumbtacks, I hung the prints until they completely covered my walls; and then I sat solemnly in the middle of the room to review what had been happening in Japan's art world since my last visit.

I was overcome by the beauty that these hard-working men had created. There was a richness and a variety that stunned me with its opulence, a warmth of comment that was constantly delightful; and I returned to the comparisons that had stung me in Mr. Abè's shop: why should my work be paid for so well and theirs so poorly? I thought: "When I consider what these men have meant to me, I'm almost obligated to do something." For some hours I pondered what to do; one could not simply share one's good fortune with no reasonable explanation, and I had already bought all the prints I could reasonably take home with me. And then an idea flashed into my mind: "Why not make a book so beautiful as to do credit to these artists? Each picture in it will be an original hand-printed work by one of them. Every penny the book earns will go back to the artists. And they'll be paid before the book is printed."

This was the proposal I made that same day to my long-time friends at the publishing house that has done more than any other in the world to introduce the Orient to the West—to Charles Tuttle, the canny Vermonter who had the foresight to expand the family business from its rare-book New England background to include a very active Tokyo publishing operation, and to his discerning Texas-born editor-in-chief, Meredith Weatherby. They studied for less than a minute before agreeing, and the fact that the book was ultimately published is due to their appreciation of what it might accomplish.

This explains the genesis of this book. But it does not describe why the book was worth doing in the first place nor the full debt of gratitude I myself, and doubtless many others, owe these artists.

It is not my intention here to write even a brief history of the artists whose work makes up this book. This has been ably done by Oliver Statler in his *Modern Japanese Prints: An Art Reborn,* which is a lively, informative essay crowded with good reproductions and was also published by Tuttle's. However, for maximum enjoyment of the prints that are to follow, it is necessary that the reader appreciate something of the historical derivation of the artists who did them and of the school that produced the artists.

Starting roughly in the middle of the seventeenth century, a group of Japanese woodblock carvers working in the two great cities of Kyoto and Edo (later Tokyo) branched out from their traditional task of carving illustrations for books and began issuing large single sheets which by themselves were works of art. Quickly the taste of the times required that these striking sheets be adorned by the addition of hand-applied colors.

Rather later than one might have supposed, sometime in the early 1700's, a device was perfected whereby colors could be applied not by hand but by block printing, but for nearly fifty years the resulting prints were limited to only two or three different colors, since registry of the colors from block to block was haphazard.

Even in these early days of the art a unique tradition characterized its technique: the artist drew the design, a woodcarver cut the blocks, a printer colored the blocks and struck off the finished prints. Invariably these jobs were done by three separate men. Sometime near 1765 the printers who worked with the famous artist Harunobu perfected a system which assured accurate registry for any number of blocks, and the great classic color prints, sometimes consisting of twenty different colors applied each from its own block, were possible. From this culminating period—roughly from 1765 to 1850—came the great names of Japanese color prints: Harunobu, Kiyonaga, Utamaro, Sharaku, Hokusai, and Hiroshige.

Magnificent work was accomplished by these men. Design was impeccable; color was subtle; execution was of a quality that has never been equaled. Starting in the 1820's, samples of the greatest previous work began filtering into Europe, and in the 1850's many leaders of the French impressionist school were already connoisseurs. The impact of Oriental prints upon the work of artists like Degas, Van Gogh, Toulouse-Lautrec, and Matisse is well known. Gauguin writes that when he fled to the South Pacific he took along a bundle of Japanese prints. Without the lessons taught by the Oriental artists, some of the innovations perfected by the impressionists might have been impossible.

But by the beginning of the twentieth century the vitality of the classical school had dissipated, and although there were skilled workmen still trying to accommodate the old techniques to the burgeoning artistic ideas of a new Japan, and although a few fine prints were still issued each year, it was apparent to all that the art of the old-style Japanese woodblock was moribund.

In the early years of the twentieth century a group of experiment-minded young Japanese decided that if their nation was to achieve a vital art, its artists would have to develop new forms comparable to those that had swept the Western world. The impact of this thinking was greatest, perhaps, in the field of oil painting, but more fruitful, possibly, in the inspired work done by a group of woodblock artists, for in this medium the best of the old tradition—fine draftsmanship, excellent design, and the world's best woodcarving—could be preserved and wedded to strong new content. One firm principle was developed: in contrast to the classical system in which the artist merely designed the print, leaving the carving of the blocks to one technician and the printing to another, the newer print artists preached that the artist himself must do the designing, carving, and printing. A new term was devised to describe such a print—*sosaku hanga,* meaning "creative print," the characters for which have, incidentally, been used as a title-page decoration and are also repeated in the watermark of the handmade Japanese paper in this book.

If one had to select one man who best exemplified these ideas, he might well choose Yamamoto Kanae (1882-1946), who studied in Japan, traveled widely in Europe, and issued a small number of prints that look as if they had been done by either Van Gogh or Gauguin. I have not seen all of Yamamoto's work, but so far I have never encountered any of his prints whose subject matter reveals that they were made by a Japanese. Almost singlehandedly he projected the modern print school into full international orbit.

The greatest artist produced by the school was Onchi Koshiro (1891-1955), a superb abstractionist who will ultimately stand beside European artists like Klee and Braque. Again, I cannot recall any of his important work that reveals in its subject matter any Oriental derivation. Onchi was an admirable artist, formed by the technical precepts of Yamamoto and the artistic impact of men like Munch of Norway, Kokoschka of Vienna, Van Gogh of Amsterdam, and Kandinsky of Berlin. His best prints are soaring poems reflecting the life of the spirit, and he set his imprint on an entire group of contemporaries.

But at the same time there were other artists who remained indifferent to Onchi's development, and these men worked out a much different approach to both art and subject matter. Hiratsuka Un'ichi, born four years later than Onchi, found that he was attracted to the simplified techniques used by the beginners of the classical school in 1650 and, using these antique processes, he began producing majestic prints in black and white. Connoisseurs quickly discovered how effective such work could be, and since Hiratsuka often chose for his subject matter the timeless architecture of Japan, his prints encouraged nostalgia.

Hiratsuka's technique was quickly adopted by the firebrand of the movement, Munakata Shiko (born 1903), whose rudely-carved Buddhist deities are the towering accomplishment of the black-and-white branch of the school. Better known abroad than Onchi, Munakata is held by most Western critics to be one of the most powerful artists working today.

After these two basic approaches to art had been established, a rich proliferation of technique and subject developed. As the prints in this book show, the contemporary Japanese print artist has the entire world of design to choose from, a subject matter that can be either traditional Japanese or *avant-garde* abstraction, a palette that ranges the entire color spectrum, and the freedom to use for his blocks any material that will yield a good impression: concrete, paper stencil, glass, realia such as leaves or shoe heels, hand rubbing, waxed paper, modern plywood, and, of course, the traditional block of cherry on which the classical prints were customarily carved.

In studying the work of this school we are watching a group of gifted artists who have been set free, who are no longer imprisoned in the conventions of one small island, and who have made themselves full-fledged citizens of the world. At the same time they remain the inheritors of a permanent tradition, and it is this interplay between the old and the new, between the inner world of Japan and the outer world of Paris, that makes the school so fascinating.

This modern school increases yearly, both in numbers and in versatility. I wish many more of its artists could have graced this volume. Aside from the ten here included and those great names already mentioned, I should like to list a few more who have particularly appealed to me; I can heartily recommend their work to the reader interested in seeing more of this exciting art:

HAGIWARA HIDEO (b. 1913) has produced a striking new kind of work which has won great favor from critics and public alike. With dark, iridescent colors superimposed upon flawless abstract design, he constructs prints that vibrate and give the impression of solid artistic control.

HASHIMOTO OKIIE (b. 1899) specializes in handsomely controlled depictions of Japan's medieval castles, done in great style, with commanding color. His prints are best when hung like Western oils.

HATSUYAMA SHIGERU (b. 1897). An illustrator of children's books, and one of the very best in Asia, Hatsuyama makes a few prints each year, but only as an avocation. They are the most poetic, the most unearthly, and the most subtly enjoyable of the work being done by the contemporaries. Like Klee, Hatsuyama has a private vision of the world, and his prints give exquisite fleeting glimpses of it.

INAGAKI TOMOO (b. 1902) has gained international notice for his highly symbolic studies of cats. An admirable draftsman, he catches the mood of nature in prints that are instantly attractive.

KAWAKAMI SUMIO (b. 1895). A wide audience has been built for his sardonic burlesques of events that occurred in Japan during the days when Europeans were first arriving with outlandish clothes and customs. These saucy prints are thoroughly delightful in a mock-archaic way.

KAWANISHI HIDE (b. 1894). His brightly colored scenes of circuses, harbor life in the port city of Kobe, and restful flower-decked interiors are marked by strong individuality both in palette and in flatness of execution. These are among the most colorful prints produced by the school.

KAWANO KAORU (b. 1916), starting much later than most of his contemporaries, began by issuing a series of prints which gained immediate popular acceptance. They show children caught up in everyday experiences yet depicted in a manner that is shot through with fantasy and loveliness. In any exhibition of contemporary prints, it is a safe guess that Kawano's portraits of children will sell first, his remarkable picture of an adorable little girl emerging from a snail's shell serving as his popular masterpiece.

KITAOKA FUMIO (b. 1918), having been born of well-to-do parents and educated in part in Paris, is probably the most sophisticated of the contemporaries. His prints excel in delicate coloring, firm control of design, and most pleasing over-all effect. He is unusual in that he works equally well in either representational or non-representational subject matter. I am very fond of Kitaoka's work and suspect that he will ultimately be judged one of the most satisfactory of the artists in this school.

MABUCHI THORU (b. 1920) has developed the most distinct technique used by any of the moderns. On flat boards he pastes little geometrical fragments of cigar-box wood until a mosaic has been built up. When blocks thus constructed are printed in strong, yet subdued, colors, the result is enchanting, a kind of pointillism in wood, a Seurat in Tokyo. His prints are big, more expensive than others, and artistically rewarding.

MIZUFUNE ROKUSHU (b. 1912). One of the most ornate styles being used today is that of Mizufune, who builds up on his prints a scintillating texture that is a delight to the eye. It has the quality of fine enamel work, but the simplicity of strong, rude art. When applied to the outlines of the fish that Mizufune often selects for subject matter, the result is positively brilliant. I am very partial to the unpredictable work of this fine artist.

NAKAO YOSHITAKA (b. 1910) specializes in powerful single figures carved with great style and with much attention to texture. They are boldly colored and create strong patterns when seen from a distance. He originally carved his blocks from wet concrete, which accounts for the striking texture of his prints, but recently he has learned to carve woodblocks so as to produce a comparable effect.

NAKAYAMA TADASHI (b. 1927). In design the prints of cranes done by Nakayama are refreshing, in carving superb, and in coloring highly individualistic, strong primary colors having been over-printed many times with flecks of subtly graded subsidiary colors until an ebb and flow is achieved which makes the print unexpectedly rich. The result is most decorative, and it is understandable why these pictures of cranes have become so popular.

ONO TADASHIGE (b. 1909). His finished work looks like a Norwegian or a post-impressionist German oil painting. Trained critics hold that his work is among the most impressive that Japan has to offer. Certainly it has more raw force than that of his colleagues, and anyone seeking diversity in his collection of Japanese prints should certainly consider Ono's work.

SAITO KIYOSHI (b. 1907) is one of those fortunate artists who have enjoyed both critical acclaim (many international awards) and also great popularity with the public (more prints sold overseas than any other modern). His powerful design, fine coloring, and interesting content covering widely scattered fields have combined to make him one of the finest working artists. Never static, he has progressed through many styles, always with distinction.

SASAJIMA KIHEI (b. 1906) has adapted the Munakata technique to the depiction of landscape, which he represents in brilliantly carved, complex, black-and-white designs. Patrons not informed in the arts usually pass Sasajima's uncompromising prints by; foreign museum directors visiting Japan for the first time almost always lug home a sheaf, for his artistic content is high.

SEKINO JUN'ICHIRO (b. 1914). One of the most successful of contemporary print artists, Sekino has issued a long series of portraits, architectural views, and theatrical scenes. One or two of the latter, in bold, twisting design, are among the best prints made in this period, his depictions of incidents in the puppet theater being the best.

SHINAGAWA TAKUMI (b. 1907). I am particularly fond of the work of this gifted abstractionist. He produces large, bright prints of great decorative value, stunning compositions with clashing colors and enormous vitality. I rarely see a Shinagawa that I do not like, and the more I keep them on my walls at home, the more rewarding I find them.

UCHIMA ANSEI (b. 1921). A native Californian but caught in Japan at the beginning of World War II, Uchima has developed into one of the subtler of the print artists. Working in an advanced nonobjective style, he creates tenuous poems in form and color which have been highly praised both in Japan and abroad.

YAMAGUCHI GEN (b. 1903) is perhaps the most international of the artists working today. His prints are of a high quality, few in number, poetic and mysterious in content. He is one of my favorites, a judgment that was confirmed when he won first prize in a world competition held in Europe. His subject matter is fantasy; his artistic mastery is superb.

YOSHIDA CHIZUKO (b. 1924). Wife of the artist who follows, this young woman has recently burst onto the print scene with an explosive series of ultra-modern compositions centering on the jazz world and its reflection in abstract art. Her prints are daringly designed and brilliantly colored. They form a distinguished if surprising addition to the Yoshida canon.

YOSHIDA HODAKA (b. 1926). Son of Hiroshi, brother of Toshi, and husband of Chizuko, this young man has a good chance of developing into the best artist of the family. He has a keen sense of design and is a fine colorist. He has vacillated between objective and nonobjective art but seems to be more at home in the latter style, in which he is continuing to produce prints of great distinction.

YOSHIDA TOSHI (b. 1911). Following in the footsteps of his distinguished father, Yoshida Hiroshi (1876-1950), who was the best-known of the traditional woodblock artists of his period and who traveled widely in the United States, Toshi has visited many parts of the world and has produced from his travels a series of handsome, interesting prints, those relating to the southwest United States being among his most effective.

It is not generally understood that often a worker in one field of the arts is indebted to men who have worked in wholly unrelated fields. Yet this is apt to be the case. To cite one obvious example, Romain Rolland could not have written *Jean Christophe* without the artistic instruction he had received from the world of music. In the field of Japanese prints Onchi Koshiro has told us of his indebtedness to European artists like Edvard Munch and Wassily Kandinsky, but he acknowledged an even greater debt to Johannes Brahms, with whom he felt a deep kinship.

My spiritual debt to the print artists of Japan is both deep and inexplicable. I was just beginning a writing career when I first met Onchi Koshiro, Hiratsuka Un'ichi, and their colleagues; so there was a freshness of morning in our association. The Japanese were older than I, more informed in the ways of art, and much more profoundly dedicated to a life of extreme hardship; but I was at a period of my development when it was of crucial importance that I encounter someone with a total commitment to the world of art, and in these Japanese artists I met such men.

I can recall my initial meetings with each of these gifted, almost childlike men. I can remember the powerful impact their work had on me, and how I derived a personal pleasure from their growth as I watched it unfold year by year, always with fresh impetus and newly invented delights. I remember with special acuity the wintry afternoon on which I first met Azechi Umetaro. The stocky little mountaineer, looking twenty years younger than his age, had just had a front tooth knocked out—how I speculated about that—and was only then beginning his adventures into the field of abstract art, which he explained to us with the fresh and winning lisp of a child. He unrolled sheaf after sheaf of new prints, and they were striking in their force and color. I startled Azechi by wanting to buy four copies of each of his latest works, because I wanted to have at hand examples of the manner in which a creative man varied his work from one printing to the next.

Later I came to know most of the artists of the school, and I acquired hundreds of their prints. There was a constant joy in returning to Japan and checking up on their accomplishment during my absence; and they, for their part, were pleased to discover what I had been doing while they were making prints. Often we dined together and I can recall one fine dinner at which some twenty of the artists convened at one of the old restaurants in the brothel section of Asakusa, where artists and intellectuals had been meeting for two hundred years, and in the flush of the night some rather expansive speeches were made. When it came my turn I said: "I won't see you for some years, but in that time you will all make a few more prints that will carry you a little closer to your goal, and I shall write a book or two which I hope will be good. We shall be a world apart, but we shall be working side by side, each helping the other."

Half of my mature intellectual life has been built around this group of men. I have written books which have helped carry their fame to the world; but I have received so much more from them than I have been able to give that at the present casting up of accounts I must owe them at least half of whatever I have been able to accomplish. Wherever I go, I keep their prints upon my wall so that I shall be constantly reminded of this debt.

It is important to record that my affection for this school of artists is neither capricious nor accidental. I did not stumble upon their prints with an untutored eye, to be bedazzled by the first bright art I saw. I served a long apprenticeship in European art and, had I had the funds when I lived so intimately amongst it, I would have collected Renoirs and Vlamincks and Chagalls and Chiricos, for my taste has always inclined that way. Also, before I saw my first contemporary Japanese print I had acquired a substantial collection of the old master-pieces done by classical artists like Utamaro, Sharaku, Hokusai, and Hiroshige. I was therefore schooled in both the best of European oil painting and the best of Japanese woodblock design.

But it was the impact of this bold new world of Japanese prints done in the full European tradition, yet combining many of the Oriental values of the past, that quite stunned me. I was at an age of my own develop-ment when I hungrily required such an experience, and it was fortunate for me that I came upon Onchi and Hiratsuka and Azechi—to name only three—when I did. I cannot specify exactly what they meant to me, what significance they held and still hold, but I suppose their impact derived from three factors. First, they refreshed my education in design, and anyone who wants to work in any of the arts had better know all about that fundamental component that he can master, for the design of a good print poses exactly the same problem as the design of a good string quartet or a decent novel. Second, these artists taught me how exciting it is to experiment in new fields and to exercise the mind to its fullest. Third, they showed me better than I had seen before or have seen since what dedication to art means.

Before these men I am contrite. A life in art for them has been so unjustly difficult, and for me so unex-pectedly easy, that a moral chasm exists between us that only contrition can bridge. I suppose that if I had been born a Japanese with an artistic drive toward the creation of excellent form and color I might have had the courage these men have had. But I cannot be sure. Therefore, since they have played so important a role in my education, I have come to think of them with envy and admiration.

This book is an attempt to express that admiration.

In the commentaries that follow, the technical information given on the page facing each print has been based on data supplied by the artists themselves. My own remarks, as will be seen, are more subjective in nature. The contest in which these ten prints were chosen is described in the concluding section of this book.

LAKESIDE AT THE BYODO-IN

by HIRATSUKA UN'ICHI

THAT one soft-spoken old man dressed in a Russian-type smock should have been able to capture in one print the essence of things Japanese must remain a miracle. Yet here in this apparently simple work Hiratsuka Un'ichi has imprisoned much of the timeless beauty that characterizes Japan.

For any print to epitomize this nature-loving country, the following components would be essential. There would have to be some kind of moving water, for Japanese will adopt any expedient to bring running water into their gardens, or even into their homes; and if the foreigner were to nominate one sound that best summarizes this land, it would have to be the soft trickling echo of water as it splashes quietly from one level to the next. This omnipresence of running water symbolizes the essential movement of nature, and its purity.

There would also have to be flowers, not conspicuously, but fitting naturally into the surroundings, for the whole emphasis of the various flower-arrangement schools that flourish in Japan is to show living things in harmonious position within a natural framework. And if the chance flower which is to appear in the print happened to be an iris, that most popular and symbolic of all the Japanese flowers, the choice would indeed be a happy one. In formal Japanese art much is made of the chrysanthemum, that bright, bold flower associated with royalty and the continuity of the empire; and as an artistic symbol the chrysanthemum lends itself to wonderful patterns. But it is sometimes overpowering; its petals fall too evenly and its colors glow too brightly. And yet the iris, growing in fragile beauty from its base of slim leaves, is the essence of Japanese art, and the print which contains such flowers is already within the great tradition.

Rocks also form an essential part of Japanese art, and whole books have been constructed showing how best to utilize rocks in gardens or in homes. Rocks, in Japan, have definite personalities and they are treasured most when they are least smooth and regular. It is the unexpected protuberance, or the intrusion of one rock composition through the heart of another, or the serrated edge that gives a rock its characteristics, and nowhere else in the world are rocks more treasured than in Japan. They speak of the timeless force of nature, the awful agelessness of the earth and its permanence. In gardens they symbolize the mountains from which Japan was formed, the powerful crags that are so dear to the citizens of this nation, the lonely aloofness of the peaks. Artists have spent much effort in depicting the nature of rocks, and there are entire series of prints which show mainly the mountains of Japan and their rocky structure. Hokusai never tired of drawing rocks, as if his strength derived from them, and today even the little-gifted artists who paint on Sundays in suburban Tokyo spend much of their hopeful effort on depicting rocks in their relationship to nature.

But water and iris and rock could be universal art symbols and are not specifically restricted to Japan. So in the middle segment of a print which was to represent the nation one would hope to find one or two symbols exclusively identified with this specific land, and none could be more appropriate than the ones Hiratsuka has here chosen: combed sand and stone lantern. The sand is extraordinary, the essence of Japan and so used only in that country. In color it is a kind of golden white; in texture rather coarser than one would find along the average beach; in quality sharper at its points than ordinary sand; and in emotional content quite unique. In Japan there are whole gardens—and the most famous—that are composed only of sand, with rocks protruding as at the left of this print. The sand is not thrown onto the surface of such gardens; it seems to grow out of them as water gushes from some deep spring. It is combed into position by the use of long rakes and is held by observers to represent the restless motion of the sea, with rock-islands such as Japan's rising from the waves. This sand is a thing of shimmering beauty. In sunlight its iridescent angles reflect points of light in the manner of a breaking sea; at dusk it is purple; at midnight a gray omniscience; and at dawn an ominous red. It is uniquely Japanese, uniquely beautiful.

The stone lantern, which is such a magnificent concept, can be used, as here, to give the central portion of any work of art a strong solidity which design often needs. The sturdy, hewn rocks, placed one upon the other in exquisite juxtapositions, yield a pattern which is instantly and constantly pleasing. Taken by itself, the typical Japanese stone lantern is one of the most immediately satisfying art forms, the heavy and oftentimes sunken base giving rise to the slender column, which is topped first by the inverted truncated pyramid, then by the hexagonal housing for the light, and finally by the stone pagoda roof. This design is one of the happiest accidents of Oriental design, except that one feels it was never an accident. From the moment I saw my first stone lantern I fell victim to its solid beauty, alas, and from time to time have carted six of the giants across the Pacific to various spots in my homeland, where they rise mysteriously from clumps of trees, or from austerely barren lawns, always with that immediately recognizable beauty which first commended them to the Japanese. I would have been much wiser to have fallen in love with polished pebbles which I could carry in my pocket, for the lanterns weigh tons, but no pebbles could convey the sense of Asian force that stone lanterns do. And it is somehow appropriate that these symbols have come to represent Japan, for it is thought that they originated in Korea, and if they did, they would thus represent one more instance in which the Japanese borrowed from neighbors only the best, and then perfected it into something better than it was when it was borrowed. In art, particularly, such borrowing from nation to nation is one of the most fruitful things the human mind can do. Only the very stupid artist fails to borrow, and certainly his chances of creating a new beauty are never good.

For the Japanese connoisseur studying this print, the five components so far identified would be merely the background for the significant content of the work. This would derive from the rich connotations of the temple glimpsed at the rear, the soaringly beautiful Byodo-in near Kyoto, with the ageless wood of its Phoenix Hall rising in serenity from nature and worship of natural gods. No need here to show the graceful phoenixes perched on the roof ridge and reflected in the water, fashioned of gold and of all man's heavenward yearnings, for they live forever in memory's eye. These planks of polished brown wood have stood on this spot for almost a thousand years. With the passing of the centuries, the temples of Japan, among which are the oldest existing wooden buildings in the world, acquire a glorious patina that reflects the sun in soft radiance. Their floor boards creak when a priest walks by, and birds nest in their rafters, making the heads of statues white with droppings. At some points the ancient wood is held together by brass or bronze fittings, and the wood seems to outlast the metal, for it accommodates itself to the seasons, growing and retreating with the sun.

These are the elements which Hiratsuka has woven into his print, and we should mark them carefully, for they bespeak the essential Japan. Here is serenity, nature at rest, the peculiar beauty of the sand and the lantern, the repose of a timeless temple, the warmth of wood and the vitality of gently moving water. Here are the works of man set down in their natural surroundings, so that one blends with the other. Here are some of the things that the Japanese artist has always sought for.

Artistically, the print is also an appropriate one with which to start a study of what is occurring in modern Japanese prints, for it is exclusively Japanese. Not a single alien component intrudes. The paper is a famous old make especially suited for prints. The ink is the same that has been used for the last two thousand years, made in the same way. The severe restriction to black and white follows the convention of the first great prints of Moronobu and his vigorous school of progenitors. Even the cutting of the wood is done with the same kinds of tools that the earliest artists used and with the same result in jagged line setting forth powerful solid areas. Technically, one can imagine this print to have been made three hundred years ago, and it is a joy to realize that what was so satisfying then remains so today.

But beyond the chance components of the print, and its technical austerity, one sees depicted here one of the secrets of Japanese art: repose and serenity achieved by the use of tension and complete control. No more appropriate print than this could have been found with which to launch this book.

HIRATSUKA UNI'CHI: *Born November 17, 1895, in Matsue, Shimane Prefecture. Resides in Tokyo. Studied Western-style oil painting at the Hongo Institute and with Ishii Hakutei and Umehara Ryuzaburo; prints, with Igami Bonkotsu. Has taught widely in Japan and, in 1943-44, in Peking; now teaches at his own institute. Has published works on print techniques and appreciation, ancient roof tiles, ancient religious folk prints, haiku, etc. Other interests include ancient calligraphy, handmade Oriental papers, Stone Age tools of Japan, and the Bunraku puppet theater.*

THE PRINT: *Artist's title:* "Byodo-in Chihan" *(Byodo-in Lakeside). Carved on a single board of* honoki *(Magnolia obovata T.) with a single flat chisel, seven millimeters wide, called an* aisuki. *Printed on* hodomura *paper from Fukui Prefecture, used raw without the usual* dosa *sizing in order to allow the sumi ink (Ryu'un from a Kyoto maker specializing in traditional ink) to sink into the paper to give depth to the print. Self-printed with many impressions of different parts (up to fifteen or sixteen for the lake area) to achieve the degree of blackness desired. The printing of each copy required about thirty minutes, with more than sixty unsatisfactory cast-offs.*

THE ARTIST'S COMMENT: *"The first idea that came to my mind in creating a print for this contest was to show a lakeside view of the Byodo-in. The impression I received when I first stood on the spot from which this print was conceived was so strong that it completely captured my heart. Hence I wanted to capture and present in the most powerful fashion that quiet moment in the afternoon when only the faint chirping of birds and the gentle rustle of falling autumn leaves could be heard. I have always believed that the motif of a print does not come through without inspiration, and that love and affection must accompany the carving and the printing. This work was created in that spirit."*

LAMP

by MAEKAWA SEMPAN

THE judges, in choosing this appealing print, could not have anticipated how important would be the role it would play in the construction of this book, for it serves as an ideal link between the classical heritage of Hiratsuka's opening print and the wholly contemporary work that is to follow.

Here Maekawa shows us a country girl holding a lamp at such an angle as to illuminate her very Japanese face. In subject matter the print is thus a pleasant combination of old and new. The face, the lamp, and the texture of the cloth are from the permanent past; the pattern of the cloth and the saucy pony-tail hairdo are definitely modern. Thus from the first glance one sees that this print represents a visual compromise.

Of special interest is the fact that the lamp throws upon the face a light which creates a masklike reflection, as if the artist had sought to convey by this subtle means the essential masklike character of the Japanese face with its large plastic forms, flat areas, and contrasting eyes. In no other country that I know have masks been so widely used as in Japan; religion and theater alike have made use of superb masks, and a collection of the historic wooden faces of the past centuries can be impressive.

That the natural Japanese face is actually masklike is of course a fallacy; it has a rather wider potential for expressive reaction than the average Western face, as a night at the Japanese theater when tragedy is being performed will demonstrate. But the traditions of Japanese life and the social necessity for controlling emotion in public have led to the forced adoption of a masklike exterior, a tendency which is reinforced by the presence of large plastic areas below the cheekbones on which the enforced calm can be mirrored.

At any rate, the mask that Maekawa puts upon his girl is an indigenous aspect of Japanese culture, and the manner in which he accomplishes it, by using one unshaded color, is doubly effective. If the color used were not flat, if it were modeled in the manner of oil painting, with shadows and contrasting pigments, the impression of a mask would not have been achieved.

In fact, the most appealing aspect of this print is its honest use of print techniques, and no work that appears in this book is more wholly within the print tradition than this. It is composed, first of all, of flat areas of color applied in large masses. The girl's hair, her face, her costume, and the right-hand shadow running down the chimney are all large masses used as they should be in print-making. The construction of the right hand is especially interesting, since it demonstrates how solid masses of color can be utilized to create the impression of form.

The shadow on the underside of the lampshade merits attention, for it illustrates how the impression of shading can be attained by using a wavering line and allowing the texture of the paper to show through. A similar use of texture explains why the sleeve of the girl's outer coat is so artistically effective, and the large flat area of the face is saved from monotony by the revelation of the texture of the paper.

It is the background of this print that creates much of the artistic interest, for the color has been applied sparingly to the block and rubbed on in such a manner that an impression of woodiness is preserved. If the background area had been printed in undifferentiated mass, it would not have sustained our interest and would have destroyed the illusion of lamplight. It is this harmonizing of technique and subject matter that makes this print so attractive by itself and at the same time so appropriate a link between the past and the present.

When, in the 1850's, the Japanese print attracted the attention and approval of the world's artists, it was because it achieved such a perfect balance between technique and subject matter. The prints looked like prints; they were the natural offspring of wood and color; they were something that could have grown to perfection only in Japan; and they exhibited a Japanese subject matter that was totally alien to the Western eye. The beautiful Japanese women depicted by Utamaro were unique to that land; the actors of Sharaku could not possibly have been Europeans; and Hokusai's imperial views of Mt. Fuji could not have been created by an artist who lived in the Alps. In fact, the more one studies the great prints of the classical period, the more impressed he is by the fact that everything about the prints—save one all-important component—was peculiar to Japan. This was what this long-hidden Oriental nation had to offer the world, and as soon as the world saw it, there was applause.

One of the main problems of this book, therefore, will revolve around the fact that only the first three prints are constructed from obviously Japanese themes with the last seven being in the international style. Many critics hold this to be lamentable; others applaud Japan's growth into full undesignated world citizenship. The reader is invited to study carefully the first three prints and to identify in them the Japanese themes that help to make them attractive. He should then try to decide for himself whether the Japanese artist is in any way obligated to adhere to such subject matter, or whether he is free to range the world in his search for theme and subject.

For example, in studying this Maekawa masterpiece the reader should observe the severe line that drops down the left-hand side of the print, from the neck of the jacket to the spot where it ends at the waist. This is artistically pleasing and fits in well with the large-mass design of the print, and Maekawa could be congratulated on having devised an attractive convention for his print; but actually this device was invented by the rare print artist Choki about the year 1790, so that anyone who knows the classic prints exclaims immediately on seeing this lovely Maekawa: "Ah! He's using the old Choki trick." Thus, in spite of its many modern aspects, this print is quite classic in its over-all impression.

One of the factors which most strongly contribute to this sense of the classic is the skilled use of line which Maekawa demonstrates. The hair is indicated in one beautiful sweep. The line from the right shoulder to the upper tip of the lamp is handsomely done and in the old style. The lovely demarcation of the face is also classical, and while the stylized nose and left eyebrow might seem at first modern, it is really only a simplification of an ancient tradition that one crisp, unbroken line must be used in prints to depict nose and eyebrow. One of the glories of the classic Japanese print was its masterful use of line that soared and swept and plunged and had a poetry of its own. In this print we catch an echo of that magisterial line, and for this reason we also exclaim: "What a classic work!"

The classicism is supported by the subdued color harmonies, by the satisfying placement of the figure off-center, and by the over-all sensation of simplicity which the print creates. It is, in a sense, a summary of all that was best in the classic Japanese print, and when critics lament the passing of that great tradition, it is prints that exhibited these appealing virtues that they are regretting.

As for this print, it falls securely within the tradition that Maekawa long ago established for himself. The subdued color scheme is his. The touch of pink has been called almost a Maekawa trademark. And the winsome little girl is a sister to the hundreds of others he depicted. He was an artist with a feminine approach to life, indifferent to the tides of modernism that have swept his colleagues, and content to look lovingly at the village aspects of a land and a society that he obviously loved.

MAEKAWA SEMPAN: *Born on October 5, 1888, in Kyoto and moved to Tokyo in 1911, where he died on November 17, 1960, shortly after receiving his prize for the present print. Graduated from the Kansai Art Academy and was self-taught in print-making. Made his living mostly as a successful illustrator but in his later years was able to devote more time to prints. His principal interests were people, prints, and visiting hot-spring resorts and folk festivals, probably in that order.*

THE PRINT: *Artist's title:* "Rampu" (Lamp). *Six blocks of Judas-tree board and basswood veneer. Printed in eight colors from Japanese pigments and poster colors on* torinoko *paper. Number of impressions not stated by the artist but presumed to be the same as the number of colors in view of Statler's remark that Maekawa liked to get each of his colors from a single heavy impression.*

THE ARTIST'S COMMENT: *"Autumn is my favorite season, particularly early autumn when the first cool days come around. In this print I fetched from my childhood memories of autumn days one of the lamps that we used to use and then perched an autumn insect on it."*

COMIC SHINTO DANCERS

by MORI YOSHITOSHI

THE two most permanent artistic forces in Japan are architecture and the dance, and of these the latter has been perhaps the more inventive and productive. I say this even though in my case it has been the architecture which has had the greater influence upon my enjoyment of the country. I love the old wooden temples that rise from the hearts of forests or cling to the sides of mountains, and I derive a constant refreshment from them. At the great shrine of Izumo in the western part of Japan, at the master shrine of Ise in the eastern, or among the ancient temples of Nara on their hillsides, I have felt that I was sharing in the permanent civilizing values that formed this island empire, for there is something timeless and universal about these gaunt old buildings and the towering trees that surround them. This is the handiwork of man at its best, the residue that lives on to give a culture its permanent base.

But I must admit that the ancient religious architecture, compelling though it may be, is static, whereas the dance, which matured alongside the shrines and temples and occasionally in them, is as vital today as it was more than two thousand years ago when its principal forms were developed. For the dance is much older than the architecture, and it is difficult to imagine any of the buildings which I love so deeply having been even started without the accompaniment of dancing. When the wooden crosstrees were first raised above the forest floor, priests danced to placate the omnipresent spirits of the wood. When important brass-studded doors were hung, priestesses danced; and throughout the life of the temple whenever an important event was about to transpire, there was dancing.

I like to visualize the superb dancing I once saw at the Kasuga Shrine in Nara, where a constantly climbing flight of many stone steps carries one to a substantial height on which the ancient shrine was built. The stairway itself is magnificent, winding as it does among tall evergreens in a kind of apotheosis of all Japanese temples, but it is enhanced by the fact that along both sides stand hundreds of the finest stone lanterns—not a dozen or so, but several hundred marching lanterns—that accompany one from the inconspicuous beginning of the stairway to its triumphal conclusion. On certain nights of the year, each of these lanterns carries its own illumination, and the forest becomes a fairyland, for the nature of the stone lantern is such that its light shoots out sharply from only a few apertures, so that night and brilliance intermingle mysteriously. And on these nights dancers approach through the lanterns and mount to the softly polished wooden platforms of the temple, and there repeat dances that must have been old when the temple was built.

It is something to see, this dancing at the Kasuga Shrine, for elderly priests move in the most stately rhythms; young priests engage in the angular, handsomely controlled postures appropriate to their age; and lovely girls in white garments that seem to remove them from earthly involvement recreate the women's dances that have always been a part of the Kasuga celebrations. Against a backdrop of towering forest and dark, soft wooden walls, these myriad dancers perform their ritual, and when one has seen this beginning he is prepared to contemplate the importance of the dance in Japanese art.

I wonder if any existing nation either accords to the dance the importance that Japan does or cultivates so many vital forms preserved over a period of twenty centuries. Today in this country one can see the most antique religious ceremonials much as they were danced even before the building of the temples. At the imperial court there are frequent exhibitions of ritualistic Bugaku dances dating back over at least a thousand years. In the classic theater one sees the Noh dance, perhaps the most highly formalized dancing any theater has ever cultivated, and in the puppet theater one finds the delightfully mechanized posturing which was so important in the development of Japanese drama and which dates back to the sixteenth century. Its origins, of course, are a thousand years more remote. In the Kabuki theater it is a rare play that does not include at least some dancing, and many consist of nothing else. How magnificent these Kabuki dances are! Since the performers are all men, there is a certain vitality to the Kabuki dance that is not seen in the theaters of other lands, but since they are also all artists, there is an extraordinary grace that differentiates the Kabuki from any other theater in the world. In costuming, in style, in control, and in vivid timeless music, this dancing provides a unique dramatic vehicle for the expression of humor, grandeur, and tragedy.

In recent years the Japanese have eagerly adopted the Western classical ballet and have performed delightfully, adapting their inherent love of dancing to the rigorous demands of international style. And in the popular theater of the young, one finds all possible kinds of dancing: wild samba, stately waltz, cardboard music-hall precision, frenetic jitterbug, and, recently, rock-and-roll and the twist. The gamut of the dance, as performed in Japan, is almost complete, and the only major form that I cannot recall having seen at one time or another is the rain dance of the American Indian. If the Japanese ever found any reason to perform this powerful dance, they would surely adopt it with an exquisite style.

Through the long history of the dance in Japan, its most brilliant moments have often been captured in prints, for theatrical subject matter has always been a major preoccupation with print artists. It has been estimated that about thirty-five percent of classical prints dealt with theatrical themes; of these, many of the finest depicted dances. Of the first ninety-seven random prints reproduced in a recent collection, twenty-three were concerned either exclusively or in large part with theatrical dances, and the great names of the art are associated with such prints: Kiyonobu, Harunobu, Sharaku, Utamaro.

It is therefore appropriate that one of the strongest prints included in this volume should be a present-day depiction of one of the oldest types of Japanese dance. Mori here shows us two oafish comedians engaged in the kind of Shinto dance that occurs at shrines like that of Kasuga as interludes between the more grave and sedate religious evocations. These comic interruptions have always been extremely popular with the common people, who must have found the hour-long religious dances somewhat tedious, for in time these ridiculous interludes gained a permanent home even in the austere Noh theater, from where they moved happily into the more robust Kabuki, where they now form one segment of almost every bill.

Who these two yokels are I do not know. Obviously they are the Oriental equivalent of Punch and Judy, of Bones and Sambo, of straight man and stooge. One feels instinctively that they are engaged in some outrageous business, for they are the timeless comedians of all who work, the necessary interruption in any well-organized theater. They are instantly recognized for what they are, and one of my most pleasant recollections in working with these prints came when a New York theatrical producer hurried through my living room, took one look at the prints here assembled, stopped before this untitled Mori and exclaimed: "Ah, the comedians! How I wish I could find a face like that one!"

As a print—here, as in the terms of the contest, I follow the Japanese usage of so classifying stencils—this is a distinguished new work in an old technique. As a conscious art form the stencil had all but died out in Japan, remaining only in such folk-art forms as the lovely *bingata* stenciled textiles of Okinawa, until revived in the present century by such men as Yanagi Soetsu, the father of Japan's now-flourishing folk-art movement, and the distinguished stencil artist Serizawa Keisuke, to both of whom Mori acknowledges a debt of gratitude for guidance.

Here the stencil's bold line and heavy mass is made a decided asset. The colors have a somber theatricality about them, and the juxtaposition of the two idiotic figures is cramped and crowded like the proscenium of an Elizabethan stage. There is a fine sense of flatness about the print, and at the same time a sensation of weight. An oil painting of these two comic actors or even a woodblock print, each with its own characteristic texture, would make them look entirely different. This is a *stenciled* print, and the relation between colors, paper, and pigment is beautifully handled. The harsh simplicity of technique is wholly appropriate. The lack of shading and the reliance upon mass is appealing, and the total impression is one of quick message, vigorously delivered.

In many respects this is a peculiarly Japanese work, for although the figures might have stepped from some rowdy passage of the Italian *commedia dell' arte,* the manner in which they are depicted is purely Japanese. The right-hand face, for example, comes straight from the puppet theater, and would be so recognized by any Japanese viewer, while the skirt and fan of the actor to the left recall both Noh and Kabuki. Then, too, the use of these particular colors is indigenous to Japan, as is the placement of the seal. This print could be as old as the dance itself. It could date from somewhere back in the eleventh century, for it is a timeless product of Japan. As such, it will be the last purely Japanese subject that we shall see in this book, and one leaves it with regret.

MORI YOSHITOSHI: *Born on October 31, 1900, in Tokyo, where he still lives. Graduated from the Kawabata Art School and studied the traditional dyeing methods of Japan and Okinawa under Yanagi Soetsu and Serizawa Keisuke, of the Japan Folk Art Association. Well known as a textile and paper designer. Principal outside interest is traditional Japanese music, particularly the short songs* (kouta) *sung to samisen accompaniment.*

THE PRINT: *Artist's title:* "Kagura no Doke" (Kagura Buffoonery). *Self-stenciled in two vegetable colors (sumi ink from pine soot and* tangara brown) on hosokawa *paper. The two stencils were made of a special paper from Shirako in Ise called* shibu-gami *(several thin layers of Japanese paper bound together with lacquer and moisture-proofed with persimmon tannin), strengthened with all-over sheets of fine-meshed cotton gauze. The black was applied two or three times and the brown three or four times to produce the desired density.*

THE ARTIST'S COMMENT: "*This work was inspired by the comic Kagura dances given at Shinto shrine festivals throughout Japan. The dancers come onto the stage, generally a roofed outdoor platform in the shrine precincts, and to the accompaniment of the traditional drum and flute give hilarious pantomimes, which are also known as fools' dances. The idea for this print came from my fond childhood memories of such fools' dances.*"

LISTENING

by WATANABE SADAO

IN commenting on this remarkable print, let me first say that the following remarks were written before I had seen the artist's comment given on the page facing the print. I have allowed my remarks to stand as originally written.

It would be difficult to find among modern Japanese prints one better calculated to illustrate the complete rupture that exists between many of the modern artists and their classical Oriental antecedents. This print could have been created by a Brazilian or an Italian or, as we shall see, a Norwegian. I dare say that even the most careful eye will fail to detect in it a single Japanese component. Boldly it announces its complete freedom from Oriental preceptors. It stands forth as a full-fledged exponent of the international style.

It is not necessarily a modern print. If one were told that it had been done two hundred years ago in Germany, one's intelligence would not automatically be insulted, and if one were told that it came from Norway eighty years ago, one would find no difficulty at all in accepting that judgment. It has a strongly medieval quality in both subject matter and style of execution. Only its clashing colors betray a modern provenance.

Artistically this print is both powerful and persuasive. The lines which depict the man are strong and harmonize well with his angular figure. They are boldly rendered, big in structure, and kept to a minimum. They have a vitality of their own and stand forth from the paper with a vibrancy which I find unusually appealing. Looked at merely as abstract design, these lines create a certain power of their own, and when enhanced by powerful color acquire added force.

One of the most commendable aspects of this work is the fact that, like its immediate predecessor, it is obviously a stencil print. The strong paper has been creatively used; the edges of the black stencil, catching stray bits of hand-applied colors in no planned manner, yield a powerful effect. Thus it is an excellent example of the dynamism that can be obtained in the stencil-print medium, and I consider it one of the finer modern prints insofar as the expression of raw power is concerned. It conveys its message quickly, dramatically, and in the high style of the earliest European graphic art.

I do not know what Japanese think when looking for the first time at this forceful, enigmatically titled print, but numerous Westerners, particularly those interested in medieval religious art, have thought they recognized one of the Stations of the Cross, with Jesus suffering on the way to Golgotha. My own reaction has been the same, not because the figure looks like Christ but because the whole effect of the print is so medieval and iconographic. If evidence were required to prove the international quality of most modern Japanese prints, I think that one's reaction to this example would clinch the case. In fact, I cannot recall any Westerner who has studied this print with me who has not volunteered the information that it depicted Christ.

How did a contemporary Japanese artist, the inheritor of one of the richest and most distinctive of all print traditions, achieve a style which so clearly negates all that went before and which at the same time throws the artist so completely into the modern world tradition? I think that the answer can be found in the first of the two masters to whom Watanabe Sadao is obviously indebted. The content and basic style of this print derive in a straight line from the inspired work of Edvard Munch, the great Norwegian graphic artist who worked in Norway at the turn of the century within a Germanic-Scandinavian tradition. He composed many powerful prints which were widely applauded in Japan about twenty years before they were discovered in America.

Munch favored subjects of brooding intensity, depicted in harsh black-and-white contrasts. His woodblocks were not carved but hacked, as if the wood had unwillingly submitted itself to an abnormal use, and the results were powerful beyond anything being accomplished in Japan at the time. Numerous Tokyo artists of that period have borne testimony to the impact of Munch's woodblocks upon their development, and his masterpiece, "Anxiety," which shows a woman fleeing some nameless fear across a bridge, had profound influence on its Japanese viewers. Several of my favorite modern Japanese prints are transparent derivations of this great Munch work.

There was something about the brooding force of Munch's approach to art that caught the Japanese love of introspection, so that whereas at first sight it might seem that the Norwegian and the Japanese had little in common, in actuality they had a great deal. The brooding winter of Norway is paralleled in much of Japan, and the extraordinary inclination to suicide that marks the one area characterizes the other also. Edvard Munch communicated instantly with the Japanese, much more so than he ever was to do with the Americans, and in Watanabe's print we see some of the results. If one grants the natural growth in color systems that Munch would surely have undergone had he lived till now, this print could easily slip into his *oeuvre* without causing complication.

If for no other reason than that here Watanabe reminds me of the forceful impact of European art on Japan, I would treasure this print. To me it is a bridge between the 1650 grandeur of Hishikawa Moronobu and the 1900 power of men like Van Gogh, Kandinsky, and Munch. I have been glad to see the Japanese artists make this transition from a purely insular tradition to a world-wide one, and although I respect the bitter recriminations of critics who feel that the Japanese have thus lost a greater heritage in trying to absorb a lesser, I cannot accept such strictures. I think it illogical to expect the artists of any one nation to live permanently outside the grand tradition of their age, and to sentence the Japanese to perpetual re-creation of the subjects and techniques that served Utamaro, Sharaku, and Hokusai so well, to forbid them to work in the newer tradition of Cezanne, Munch, and Picasso, makes no sense at all to me. If American artists like Jackson Pollock and William de Kooning and German artists like Franz Marc and Max Beckmann are free to work through the international tradition until they find their own strong style, then surely the Japanese must be accorded the same courtesy. No critic has a right to deny them this experience.

But what the critic does have a right to insist upon is that when the Japanese artist sets forth to conquer the international style he must not abandon completely the Japanese heritage which gave him his artistic impulses in the first place. It would be ridiculous, argue such critics, and with justice, for a Japanese print artist to forget or ignore the work of his predecessors, for no nation ever developed a happier wedding of blocks and paper and color than that worked out by the Japanese in the two centuries between 1650 and 1850. If one respects the warnings of critics who so argue, and I certainly do, then one expects to find in the modern Japanese print at least some acknowledgment of the great heritage that helped form the artist.

And that is the second reason why I like this print: it owes three great debts to its Japanese past. First there is the old stencil technique already discussed in my remarks on Mori's "Comic Shinto Dancers." Second is the application of colors by hand, a technique used early in the history of the Japanese woodblock print, though here employed, as it were, in reverse, with the black applied last rather than first.

And, thirdly, the print cries loudly, from the first moment one sees it across a room, of its debt to the second of Watanabe's masters, the foremost living Japanese print artist, Munakata Shiko, whose stark black-and-white masterpieces have received world acclaim. They are well known in America, whose museums own many examples, and their importance as the best of modern graphic art has long been acknowledged. Munakata works mostly in the style originated by Moronobu, that is, powerful single figures set forth on white paper by means of gashing lines; but he also issues sets of prints in which color is added by hand. The relationship between Munakata and Watanabe will be immediately apparent to anyone who knows the work of the former.

Thus this powerful, awkward print combines in its harsh lines and glaring color the two strands of inheritance that have made the modern print of Japan: the instruction from Edvard Munch, who represented the best of Europe, and the timeless force of Munakata Shiko, who springs in direct line from the original power of Hishikawa Moronobu and more particularly from the nameless Buddhist artists who carved powerful iconographic figures which were printed in editions of many thousands for use at temples in the tenth century and onward. It is this harmonization of two great traditions that makes this print so important, and the modern connoisseur can well test his reaction to graphic arts by studying this Watanabe figure that seems so much like a medieval Christ.

WATANABE SADAO: *Born July 7, 1913, in Tokyo, where he still lives. No formal art education but, like Mori Yoshitoshi, received guidance from Yanagi Soetsu. Winner of several Japanese art awards. Textile designer. Lists his other interests as "plants and animals."*

THE PRINT: *Artist's title: "Kiku" (Listening). Self-executed in natural mineral and vegetable pigments in the following stages: First, red background applied to the entire paper surface with a wide brush. Second, white, green, and yellow colors applied by hand with a brush. Third, black overprinted in one impression by means of a stencil of* shibu-gami, *the same stencil paper used by Mori Yoshitoshi for the preceding print. The paper used for the printing surface is a variation of the* kozo *type called* momi-gami (*crumpled, wrinkled paper*); *its texture is produced by crumpling up the paper by hand and then only partially smoothing it out.*

THE ARTIST'S COMMENT: *"I have always aspired to portray stories and episodes from the Bible. In this disturbed world, I would like to be able to heed the voice of Heaven. The person shown in this print is no one in particular but was created in this spirit. Being somewhat reluctant to comment on my own work, I have jotted these words down here in this simple fashion for whatever help they may be in preparing a commentary."*

1960 SADAO WATANABE 22/51

FACES

by KINOSHITA TOMIO

IN 1957 the hitherto unknown woodblock artist Kinoshita Tomio, then thirty-four years old, startled artistic Tokyo with a series of large prints consisting of stylized human heads depicted in a striking new manner. Usually only black and one color were used, and those subdued, but both critics and buying public found the results immensely to their liking, and a new artist was launched.

The chief characteristics of Kinoshita are well exemplified in this work, which is composed of severe geometrical patterns sensitively tied together into a pleasing design. The blocklike heads dominate the body of the print, but subsidiary geometrical patterns are utilized, as in the isosceles triangle that forms the chin of the left-hand face and the right-angled triangle that forms the hair of the right-hand head. The viewer is invited to find the other geometrical patterns for himself, and to see how cleverly they are juxtaposed in order to obtain maximum artistic effectiveness.

But the chief characteristic of the prints is the jagged line which the artist uses to convey the sense of grain in the wood. Many purchasers of these prints have assumed that the artist has gouged out the soft pith of the wood, obtaining his black printing lines from the remaining hard ridges of the grain. Even the most cursory inspection will prove that this was not the technique, but that each black line was skillfully carved and that what seems to be the essence of the wood is nothing but an artistic invention which, as so often happens, turns out to be superior to realism.

One can have only admiration for the masterly manner in which Kinoshita compresses his black lines in order to obtain the sensation of eyes and mouth. Shading is also adroitly suggested and heads given weight by a fine use of plastic forms. Much less effective would such prints be if the background were not kept starkly simplified, as shown here.

In some of his most appealing prints Kinoshita has used not the harshly angular edged squares shown here but elliptical heads posted on columnar necks. These yield delightful pictorial results, with severe concentrations of lines forming dark parallels to indicate eyes and mouth and vertical concentrations for the nose and chin. But attractive as these ellipses are, it is the square-cut heads that produce the stronger effect of woodiness, which is so appropriate to this technique. On the debit side, the square-cut heads seem a little more obvious and artistically transparent, whereas the elliptical heads come closer to nature and therefore shock the viewer less. But in spite of their obviousness, the square-cut heads seem to be preferred by most collectors.

Since Kinoshita's technique stresses the feeling of wood, it has revitalized an old delusion that has plagued sculptors for many years. Some observers have said of these prints: "The heads seem to grow out of the wood, as if the idea had been lying dormant in the oak." Sculptors are always hearing admirers praise them for having "set free the innate characteristic of the rock."

I find such animistic nonsense repugnant in that it contradicts the essential nature of art, which is that the mind of the artist can use inanimate materials and by bending them to his will, but always within the natural capacities of the materials, can externalize his concepts. That either wood or stone should have within it some innate intellectual content which the artist mysteriously releases is insupportable. Kinoshita's wood carried with it no dormant concept of the simplified heads he has been able to obtain with his knife. Those heads sprang from Kinoshita's head and are a tribute to his conceptual powers alone.

It could be argued, I suppose, that Kinoshita's carving of one wood to make it look like another is artistic trickery and that it somehow perverts the natural characteristic of the wood. To appreciate what I am discussing, the reader should at this point turn to the next print, Shima Tamami's study of birds, which represents one of the most exquisite uses of wood seen in any modern print. In Shima's work the judgment of the artist as to her material was without flaw, and she accommodated her design to the natural structure of the wood in a manner which makes her print a superb work of graphic art.

In Kinoshita's print, on the other hand, the artist's jagged line in no way grows out of the panel onto which it was carved. It is an arbitrary line, arbitrarily carved for an arbitrary purpose. Put another way, Kinoshita has not accommodated his concept of the future print in any way to the natural limitations of the wood. Any wood which had the relationship of pith and hard ridge suggested by this print would be wholly unsuitable for carving. Interestingly enough, it would be particularly unsuitable for carving the print that Kinoshita has carved. To achieve this sense of oaken people, stalwart on their land, the artist required a wood as much unlike oak as possible, so that the sentimental concept of the artist's somehow releasing the spirit of the wood is sheer non-sense. Any artist who "releases the innate spirit" of an average piece of wood is going to get a very poor print indeed, for the essential component of great art will be automatically lacking: the operation of a human mind on the materials at hand.

Therefore, much as I shall praise the next print when I come to it, I must say here that I prefer Kinoshita's method of cutting blindly across the heart of his material, rather than Shima's contrasting method of adjusting herself to the idiosyncrasies of her wood. In any given print, the Shima method has a good chance of producing the more acceptable work, and I suppose that in the case of this Kinoshita and the following Shima, the latter is the finer print; but in the long run the method adopted by Kinoshita—that of hammering his materials into a form that will adjust to his concept—will be the one with much chance of producing great art.

In looking at Kinoshita heads one has a feeling of the music of Jean Sibelius, an authentic, hard, composed line of melody hewn with difficulty from all the available sounds. There is much selection and conscious choice in the art of these two men, and each is characterized by an avoidance of cliché.

Many viewers have found in these heads, particularly the elliptical ones, an echo not of Sibelius but of the American regional painter Grant Wood, whose "American Gothic" and "Daughters of Revolution" have been composed of similar lines and plastic values. Certainly, one would here look in vain for any telltale sign that these heads came from Japan. Not even in the use of line, color, or paper do I find any indication that this print stems from the great Japanese tradition.

This is a free art. It could have been produced in any of the world's major areas. In style it is perhaps closer to the German tradition than any other, for it obviously could have been created by a Dürer or perhaps a Leo-nardo. It is much closer to them than it is to the Japanese draftsman Utamaro as his style is exemplified in his books of natural and scientific drawing.

From the moment of Kinoshita's initial appearance I have been partial to his prints, for they convey a sense of great simplicity and force, a combination which often produces enviable art. They have a universal quality, for as I have pointed out they could be of Renaissance derivation, yet they also represent the stoic modern man set grimly against an age he does not fully comprehend or approve. Weak though they may be when confronted with forces of darkness, these men display stubbornness and courage, characteristics which are perhaps more easily detected in the square-block figures than in the elliptical ones.

What I am trying to say is this: I like these prints for the same reason I like Richard Wagner. When one first sees them, as when one first hears Wagner, one knows that an artist has been trying to convey a conclusion which was important to him. These prints are art. They are not pictures of pretty people, or records of a con-versation, or the imprisonment of trivia. They set out to be art, and their intention is immediately recognized. For that reason I like them.

KINOSHITA TOMIO: *Born January 10, 1923, in Yokkaichi, Mie Prefecture, where he still lives. Graduated from the Nagoya School of Industrial Arts; self-taught in print-making. Lists his hobbies as books, movies, and sports.*

THE PRINT: *Artist's title: "Kao 3" (Faces, No. 3). Carved on two Judas-tree boards and printed on natural-color torinoko paper. Self-printed, with carmine and vermilion water colors mixed to obtain the orange, which was impressed three times; sumi ink used for the black, impressed twice.*

THE ARTIST'S COMMENT: *"A full title for this print would be 'Faces of the Weak Courageously Attempting to Move Forward in a World of Darkness.' This is one in a series of prints I have been working on for four or five years, all having the common motif of faces or masks. In combinations of faces such as the present I am trying to express the sufferings of society, of man, of mankind, of all living beings. I am not too certain of my results: perhaps in the end I have produced mere 'prints.'"*

BIRDS

by SHIMA TAMAMI

FROM the moment the prints in this contest were assembled, both critics and general public nominated one as pre-eminent. This lyric, exciting work by Shima Tamami has an immediate appeal which does not diminish with familiarity. In color it is quiet and satisfying, each of its individual tones blending with the whole and each impressing the viewer as being appropriate to the subject. The use of wood in graphic art is nowhere in this series better exemplified than here, while the carved line is both artistically pleasing and technically expert.

But what gives the print its inviting charm is the subject matter, a handsome, stylized scene from nature in which the three birds are splendidly varied in their attitudes, yet artfully disposed to produce a well-designed print. The brief suggestion of a woodland that runs through the middle background of the print is cleverly done, while the contrast between sky and water is beautifully achieved.

This is a most adroit print, and I doubt if a better could have been found to illustrate in one brief example why it is that the modern Japanese print has been found so appealing by so many connoisseurs. The simplification attained in this work is admirable, but the depth of joy that shows through that simplification is one of the finest things that art can accomplish. I cannot imagine anyone's tiring of this rhythmic, plastic work, and if the reader should want a fine example of what the print form can achieve, this print would be the answer, for it is an almost perfect work.

There are many aspects of this print that will repay close study, but I should like to deal with only three: design, texture, and use of wood.

Start with the outermost extremities of the bills of the three birds, and see how, beginning with the one farthest away, the tips stand each at a similar distance from the top and the right-hand side of the paper's edge, a distance which is repeated with the bottom and tail of the foremost bird. These points, taken in sequence from upper left, across the top of the print and down the foremost bird's extended neck and around to his tail, form the outside rhythmic pattern inside which the body of the print is confined. The three-quarter circle thus subtended is broken twice, once by the arbitrary intrusion of the band of woodland scene that cuts the right margin just below the middle, and again by the tail of the middle bird. When I first saw this print I liked the use of the bird's tail to break the rhythm very much, but I thought the use of the light band somewhat arbitrary; now that I know the print more intimately, I see that Shima was correct and that without that bold cutting of the pattern, the circle would look rather obvious.

To continue the discussion of the design, the placement of the three birds within the circle seems inspired. What differentiation the artist achieves, what variation in weight and balance, what a superb utilization of line to create form and implied movement! The three postures of the bills are a little obvious, I am afraid, but the extremely bold invention of the forefront bird in contorted sweep is something that most of us would have been quite incapable of. If the three bills are to be questioned as obvious, certainly that wild bird in front must be warmly commended as excellent artistic invention.

The manner in which the dark lower portion of the rear bird, as it intersects the band of forest, assumes the focal point of interest is likewise admirable; a lesser artist would have had his center of interest much higher and would thus have lost the relationship between the rear bird and the dominant forefront one. And the manner in which the middle bird ties the whole interior design together is commendable. The rhythm obtained by these various devices is positively insidious, for the beholder's eye keeps sweeping round and round this picture, like a bird in flight.

One of the most attractive elements in this print is the varied texture, divided into five contrasting types. There is the soft fleecy effect of the sky, achieved by utilizing one distinct kind of wood creatively. There is the rippling texture of the water, achieved by using a different wood quite differently. There is the neutral texture of the band of forest which heightens the contrast between sky and water. There is the glossy texture of the solid black portions of the birds. And there is the very effective mottled texture on the backs of the first and second birds, obtained from a paper block printed in black over blue.

One would be most naive to assume that these contrasts were accidentally obtained. That they were so adroitly managed is a tribute to the artist, but also a reminder of how important texture has become in many modern Japanese prints. In this print the textures are tactile. One can feel with his forefinger the different effects Shima is after. In Kinoshita's "Faces" the texture is implied. In the print before that, Watanabe's mysterious figure of a man, the texture derives from the rough paper and the even rougher application of colors. Three other artists not represented in this book who specialize in superb texturing of their prints are Mizufune, Nakayama, and Ono. Sometimes even to see the contrasts they obtain is pleasing, regardless of the subject matter of the print.

But few prints, even those by artists who have stressed this aspect of art, have equaled Shima's use of texture as evidenced in this print, and much of the attractive quality which marks this work stems from its real and implied textures. Graphic art which ignores this problem today foregoes one of its richest components.

The most distinctive aspect of this print, however, is its use of wood. On pieces of plywood, which is now customarily used by Japanese artists since the original cherrywood block has proven too small and too hard for the effects the modern artists desire, Shima found, for the upper half of her background, a widely spaced, freely moving grain that resembled clouds and, for the lower, a rippling and more tightly spaced grain to suggest water. With special pigments that emphasize the grain of the wood, she has obtained printing surfaces capable of re-creating two quite distinct effects. The band of different texture thrown across the meeting line of the two woods was brilliantly conceived and eliminates what might otherwise have been a rather transparent device: the harsh juxtaposition of the sky and water.

Shima's use of the broad-sweeping grain in the upper half of her print was by no means a modern invention. It was used with marvelous effect as early as 1750 by the classical artist Ishikawa Toyonobu, who did several prints with such backgrounds, and in 1765 by Suzuki Harunobu, who designed one of his masterpieces, a dancer with a monkey, with a similar marbled background. In later works, especially those by Katsukawa Shun'ei and Utagawa Toyokuni, some designs, while not actually emphasizing the exposed grain of the wood, did strive after somewhat similar effects by pressing the printing *baren* so harshly upon the wetted paper as to leave printing marks on the larger background areas. Such marks were held to be artistically desirable, in that they reminded the viewer that the print had sprung from a block of wood.

And here we are right back where we were in our reflections upon the preceding print, where Kinoshita Tomio carved an ordinary piece of wood so as to impart the sense of oak to his print. Here Shima Tamami has done just the opposite; she has searched for sheets of plywood which were so fortuitously constructed that they could hardly help but impart to their print a real sense of woodiness. Without in any way denying the beauty and power of Shima's results, of the two artistic techniques I still prefer Kinoshita's. I have already, in my remarks on his "Faces," given my rationale for this judgment. So in all fairness to Shima I should also admit to a subjective and quite irrelevant prejudice.

Japan has always had a group of craftsmen who search for *tsuga* (spruce-hemlock) wood of interesting texture. They char it in a fire, then rub away the burned pith, leaving myriad little black ridges against a handsome dark-brown underpith. From such wood these men carve the cleverest hoptoads, in which the alternate strata of black ridge and uncharred pith are made to look like a frog's skin with warts. Tourists seem to love these frogs, but I find the damned things repulsive, a *reductio ad absurdum* of the Japanese love of wood which is here so appealingly expressed by Shima.

SHIMA TAMAMI: *Born in Aomori Prefecture, August 11, 1937; now married to another print artist and living in Tokyo. Graduated from Tokyo Women's University of Arts.*

THE PRINT: *Artist's title: "Tori B" (Birds B). Six plywood blocks (lauan, basswood, and* sen *or Kalopanax ricinifolius M.) and, for the black striations on the backs of two of the birds, one paper block made by untwisting paper string and pasting the crepe-textured paper on a board. Self-printed on Takasago* torinoko *paper in three colors of special oil pigments from which the oil was removed in order to bring out strongly the grain of the wood. About two impressions for the light areas and about five for the dark. Several of the blocks had to be made anew during the course of the printing, resulting in different grain patterns between one print and another.*

THE ARTIST'S COMMENT: *"I have worked with the bird motif ever since I first took up prints. In the composition of the present print I treated the birds as still-life objects. I am not completely satisfied with this print because of its small size."*

MOUNTAINEER IN SNOW

by AZECHI UMETARO

THIS dramatic print represents a dividing line between the first six works, which are representational in content, and the last three, which are not. Of the representational works, only the first two could possibly be called copies of nature and even these escape such a category because of their high artistic purpose and their inventive utilization of form, material, and carving.

Before attempting to appraise this Azechi snowman, standing as he does between the representational and the nonrepresentational, the reader would be wise to restudy those first prints in order to determine for himself what his preferences are regarding the subject matter of art, and particularly the subject matter of modern Japanese art; for many critics have warned that the Japanese have moved too far and too radically toward a nonrepresentational theory of art and that in doing so they have discarded those very elements of design and content which made their national art strong in the first place. Some of these critics have argued further that the Japanese classical heritage is so strong in modern Japan that artists reared in this tradition cannot properly absorb the international style and are thus condemned to mimicry of Western forms without ever achieving any understanding of their underlying significance.

Many who seriously concern themselves with the future of Japanese art decry experiments like those we are about to inspect as psychological aberrations produced by men who have lost contact with their own heritage without finding a secure footing in an alien tradition. Rarely has this fear been better expressed than by Georgia O'Keeffe, who once said, after studying a portfolio of contemporary Japanese prints: "These men have sacrificed the traditional Japanese line, color, control, and subject matter without inventing anything to take their place." Other critics have suggested that the best the Japanese artist can hope to achieve by dedicating himself to international styles is an ineffective copy of work being done in Paris, lacking distinctive form, emotional content, or those Japanese subject matters which up to now have so enchanted the world.

I suspect that much of the criticism of contemporary Japanese prints stems from this last consideration, this yearning on the part of Western critics and buyers for the old familiar subject matter made famous by Utamaro, Sharaku, Hokusai, and Hiroshige. When the Western connoisseur has taken the trouble to make the intellectual jump which permits him to accept the distorted heads of Sharaku, the ethereal ladies of Utamaro, and the unusual landscapes of Hokusai and Hiroshige, he is not entirely happy when the successors to these artists abandon what he has grown to like and commit themselves instead to an entirely different body of subject matter, one which, moreover, he can find abundantly in either Paris or New York. Whether they know it or not, these critics are telling Japanese artists: "We have grown to expect from you familiar subject matter taken from the world of the geisha, the Kabuki actor, and the traditional view of Mt. Fuji. Don't disappoint us. Keep on doing what you have always done so charmingly."

I find nothing wrong with such an admonition, and I suppose that that was what Miss O'Keeffe really meant when she decried the contemporary incursions into alien subject matter. We all grew to love the older subject matter; let the artists therefore keep providing it to us and we shall all feel more comfortable. But there is a corollary to this intellectually admissible injunction, and it is not admissible. This corollary says: "It is all right for a Spaniard like Picasso or Dali to work in the international style. Or a Frenchman like Leger or Dufy. Or an American like Rothko or Pollock. But it is not fitting for a Japanese like Azechi or Yoshida Masaji to do so. They are somehow mysteriously Japanese and must therefore continue to work in the old manner and with the old subject content." I find no logic in this admonition.

It is true that a Japanese classicist like Hiratsuka Un'ichi will produce good work, as he did in the first print in this book, when he keeps to the strict tradition of an inherited art, and he would probably be a fool if he were to abandon what has for him become second nature; but it is also true that a modernist like Yoshida Masaji, whose work we will encounter shortly, finds almost no point of contact with traditional Japanese subjects and styles. He is at home in the intellectual and artistic ambience of Paris and New York; he has a right to find his companionship there; he has a right to work out his destiny in terms similar to those that have developed men like Picasso and Leger. I therefore find that even though I have spent a good many of the pleasure hours of my adult life working in the field of the classic Japanese print, when I come to decorate my own home I prefer the nonrepresentational modern print almost four to one. Had I been the judge of the contest which produced this group of ten striking prints, I would have chosen about three representational prints and seven like those we are about to inspect. Those are my tastes. But I suppose that the judges did us all a service in inclining the other way, because if we follow their more gradual introduction we are better prepared to consider this paramount problem of art; by moving cautiously from Hiratsuka and Maekawa and on to the vigorous moderns we grow to appreciate what a print can accomplish today, its manifold richness of tradition, its capacity to speak in many tongues.

I have therefore come to the conclusion that the judges were well advised in their balance between representational and nonrepresentational. They were shrewder in their selections than I would have been, for they have provided both a better balance and a better unfolding emotional experience than my more radical choice would have permitted. But having admitted this, I must then confess with what joy I come to this Azechi print and its introduction into the world of the brilliant *avant-garde* work being done today in Japan.

To one who knows something of the development of this school, there could be no better gateway print than this snowman of Azechi's, for it recapitulates in the compass of one brilliant work the ontogeny of the school. Azechi began his art career by producing literal scenes of the ocean and of city life. They were satisfactory, but not distinguished, and some of the prints of this first period have the characteristics of picture postcards. Through the accident of becoming interested in mountain climbing—he is now one of Japan's foremost alpinists—he started carving a second type of print: a series of mountain scenes in which the massive formations of the Japanese peaks stand forth in marvelous simplicity. Usually these prints, which made him famous, show no human beings, a few trees or none, and receding masses of rock and snow. They are at once both fine representational art and the beginning of the artist's search for controlled form. Of them Azechi says: "Most of my mountaineering friends don't like these prints. Their love for the mountains is very literal, and they strongly object that I change the forms of the peaks in my prints."

Established as a fine if arbitrary landscapist, Azechi surprised his friends by launching a third type of print: rugged, simplified, idealized portraits of mountain men, and these are among the most striking and immediately accepted of all contemporary Japanese prints. Against a starkly blue sky rise a few stylized peaks, some black, some covered with white snow. Filling the foreground of the print rises a figure clad in mountaineering togs and obviously a man, yet in such severely stylized form that he has come to look like a cylinder with feet, no legs, angular arms, and a boldly formalized face. The accoutrements of mountain climbing, often depicted in a brilliant green, add a garish yet evocative touch. These are brilliant prints and when they first appeared Azechi's admirers said: "He has found himself." His detractors pointed out: "He has lost the man in the mountains."

When I first saw examples of Azechi's third type I intuitively felt: "These are a way station. I'd better acquire all that I like, because he won't be making these for long."

It is with unusual personal interest, therefore, that I greet his fourth style of print. His present snowman is the lineal descendant of those first vivid portraits that captivated the public a dozen years ago. Clearly the roughly indicated mountain backgrounds are echoes of the fine prints of his third period. But what has happened is a thing of great importance: like old-man Titian, like pre-death Van Gogh, like octogenarian Giuseppe Verdi, my dear and cherished friend Azechi Umetaro is searching for a more simplified artistic expression. And to watch this evolution is a thing of wonder. One holds his voice and halts his breathing, for to see an artistic idea evolve is one of the rarest experiences a human being can share.

AZECHI UMETARO: *Born December 28, 1902, in Ehime Prefecture, on the southern island of Shikoku; now lives in Tokyo. After graduating from elementary school, worked for two years as a merchant seaman before turning to art. Received instruction at different times from Kobayashi Mango and Hiratsuka Un'ichi and, later, from Onchi Koshiro and Maekawa Sempan. Worked for the government printing office for three years and also spent a year in Manchuria. Also does illustrations and writes. Loves mountain climbing.*

THE PRINT: *Artist's title:* "Yuki-otoko" (Snowman). *Seven plywood blocks of basswood and lauan: two for the background, two for the black, one each for the white, red, and purple-red. Six colors of Japanese* gouache *printed on* kozo *paper from Fukui Prefecture sized with* dosa. *Background printed in two impressions, one vertical and the other horizontal; two impressions each for the black and the white; one impression each for the other colors.*

THE ARTIST'S COMMENT: *"Here I tried to express not only the natural beauty of mountains but also the relationship of man and mountain. By the title I am referring to a simple mountaineer who walks the mountains in winter."*

WINTER COMPOSITION

by IWAMI REIKA

THIS print is special in many ways. First of all, it was done by Miss Iwami Reika, the first woman in the history of Japanese prints, so far as I know, to attain full stature. It is true that Hokusai's daughter, an extraordinary girl known by the name of Chin-chin because her protruding jaw reminded one of the Pekinese dog (called *chin* in Japanese), issued a few works that gained wide circulation in the middle years of the nineteenth century; but she was never really much more than a curiosity, and her work was in no way commendable. It is also true that today there are other fine women print artists who are gaining increasing recognition—Shima Tamami and Yoshida Chizuko, to name only two—and that there are now enough of them to have an informal association and to hold periodic exhibits of considerable worth. But Miss Iwami represents the vanguard, and for two women to win prizes in a competition such as the present one signalizes a triumph of no small proportion. It has never been easy for women to attain prominence in Japanese art, and for two such young ones to have done so is indeed an accomplishment.

More important, artistically, however, is the second fact: this print exhibits a mastery of texture and color that is enviable. The utilization of wood grain in the three standing pillars is very satisfying and gives the print a surcharge of emotion. The printing of this passage and also of the background grays is first rate, skillful overprinting being used to bring out unanticipated textures. In others of her prints, Miss Iwami uses a striking palette of burnt orange, crisp yellow, and flashing red. Here she is more subdued, but her vivid sense of color values nevertheless expresses itself in the telling slash of red across the moon.

The third reason why this print has a special significance in this series is that it exemplifies rather handsomely the best effects that are being obtained by the nonrepresentational artists in simplifying subject matter to the ultimate. What more need be said about winter in Japan, where the wonderful texture of the unpainted wooden houses stands so starkly against the cold sky? The resulting patterns are most satisfying, emotionally, and many people who have had an opportunity to live closely with others of Miss Iwami's prints can testify to the subtle gratifications one discovers in having them around. They are somehow right; both the eye and the mind find them recurrently pleasing, and thus they satisfy one of the great purposes of art: they remind us of how simple the most effective measures usually are. Miss Iwami utilizes simple means, simple design, simple, bold coloring, and out of this produces a complex, sophisticated whole that has the capacity to please without cloying.

The final characteristic of this print that makes it special for me is that it was done by an artist whom I had the pleasure of helping discover. All the men represented in this book were well-established performers before I came on the Tokyo scene. Hiratsuka was producing fine prints before I was born, and Maekawa too. Azechi was well into his third period—the portraits of mountaineers against stylized peaks—before I met him; and each of the other artists was well known. But Iwami Reika was not.

I can recall the day on which I was passing an art store in Tokyo and saw a copy of the first print that Miss Iwami was offering to the public. At the time I supposed the artist was another of the gifted young men who were knocking for admission to the ateliers of critical review, and I remember thinking: "That one might make it." But as I was about to pass by, I stopped to restudy the beautiful use of texture which characterized this unknown print, its vivid yet controlled coloring, and its wholly satisfying composition. I concluded then that this Iwami, whoever he was, had already reached a point rather more advanced than competing artists who were just then appearing on the scene, and I went inside to make inquiries.

The man in charge did not then know that Iwami-san was a woman, but he did have two other samples of the artist's work, and I bought all three. I took them back to my hotel, where the well-known Texas artist David Adickes was visiting with me during an art trip around the world. We hung the three Iwami prints and sat back to decide whether or not I had been misled in my enthusiasm. We called in others to help us in our judgment, and the result was not entirely reassuring. Adickes said bluntly: "Looks to me as if a woman had done them, and she lacks strength." The thought had not occurred to me, and I protested: "No woman did those prints. The control is too evident."

The more I kept the three prints before me, the more I grew to like them. The attributes that I had liked originally increased in merit: texture, control of design, color, emotional satisfaction. I convinced myself that Mr. Iwami was destined to be an artist. I therefore set out to find what I could about his life and his working habits.

To my surprise I found that David Adickes was right. Iwami-san was a young woman who had arrived on the Tokyo art scene, by the way of doll-making, with a roll of prints, and everyone who had seen them had been impressed. They were not yet perfect prints, and some critics thought she would never attain perfection, but she won encouragement and a few sales.

At big shows I began to spot her work, and it maintained its high standards. Her coloring improved, if anything, and her sense of spacious design continued to provide her with subject matter that caught the mind's eye. She was on her way, and I felt an inward glow of satisfaction.

One day, on a crowded street off the Ginza, I was stopped by an earnest young woman of no particular appearance. I can't recall now whether she wore glasses or not. It was midwinter and she was well bundled up in the Japanese manner. I seem to retain the impression of a girl somewhat taller than average and not at all bad looking. She knew almost no English and I no Japanese, but she said "Aren't you Mr. Michener?" and I replied that I was. She said that she appreciated the interest I had taken in her work, and I told her that I was convinced she would one day be a most commendable artist. We bowed, then bowed again and started to go, but I took her by the hand in the American manner and shook it warmly, saying: "I'm sure you're going to be very good, Iwami-san. Keep working." She could not have understood what I was saying, but it was obvious that she knew.

How pleased I was, some years later, to discover that the judges of the competition had nominated not one of her lovely prints, but two. Despite her own personal preference as stated in her comment, to me the one shown here seems the more complete work of art.

IWAMI REIKA: *Born March 27, 1927, in Tokyo; now commutes from near-by Kawaguchi, Saitama Prefecture. After graduating from high school, worked in the medium of creative doll-making before turning to prints. Studied print-making in Sunday classes at the Bunka Academy. Employed in the office of the Athénée Francais, a language institute. Other interests include music and horticulture.*

THE PRINT: *Artist's title: "Fuyu no Kosei 2" (Winter Composition No. 2). Four plywood blocks of basswood and lauan. Printed on torinoko paper in three Japanese-style pigments plus sumi ink, with mica and gum arabic mixed into the black and red. Two impressions for the gray background and one impression each for the black, the thick red, and the thin red.*

THE ARTIST'S COMMENT: *"This is one of two prints by the same title; I personally prefer the No. 1. Since the deadline for the contest was the last day of December, I picked the theme of winter for my compositions. It was partly with a feeling of resistance against the cold and cruel impression of winter that I worked on these prints. What I wanted to express, however, was that even though winter is cold and severe, it is at the same time secretly nursing the buds of hope."*

EARTH

by YOSHIDA MASAJI

DESPITE the artist's title for this print, it is so instinct with the essence of Japan and stands in such peculiar relationship to the artist and his emotional history that the Western observer feels impelled to find a more appropriate title; I myself think of it as "The World of Zen." Through a contemplation of this print one can attain, I think, a better sense of what the contemporary artists are after than in any other way.

Masaji—he is usually called by his given name to differentiate him from the other five distinguished Yoshidas, all members of one print-making family, to whom he is unrelated—is the most intellectual of the print artists, a man of exquisitely refined tastes who has been encouraged by a small coterie of admirers to pursue his highly individualistic art. He makes his living teaching in public schools, for his prints have never sold in large enough quantities to support him, and his influence is widely felt in the school system.

His mysterious prints, for it would be impossible to describe them in any other way, fall into four clear categories, of which the present is properly the capstone. At the end of the war, when he found destruction throughout his city and color running wild in the paintings of his friends, he retreated to a severely cauterized world of gray marked by symbolic figures. These prints were distinguished by an autocratic control which stood in contrast to the chaos he saw and felt about him. They are handsome works, large and clean and impressive.

From this concept he soon progressed to an even more austere vision of the world, which he depicted in a series of brilliant, immense prints titled *The Fountain of Earth.* These consist of rigidly disposed series of straight black-and-white lines dominated here and there by large black or white circles. They are stunning prints, some of the most dramatic ever to have been released in Japan, and as decoration they are superb. They command attention wherever they are displayed, and since they stand about two feet tall by three feet wide they exhibit a kind of gigantism that adds to their effectiveness. I am extremely fond of these prints, for as effective pure pattern they are most compelling, and the harsh contrast of black and white gives them a vitality that other more vividly colored prints lack. They have not been popular with the public, and few Americans own copies, an oversight that ought to be corrected while good printings are still available.

Masaji's third kind of print formed a radical departure and was occasioned, as such new forms ought to be, by a personal crisis within the conscience of the artist. The prints appear mostly in purple and black and always with a swarm of closely knit lines such as one sees at the top of the Masaji print shown here. The designs are tortured, involuted, brooding, and the mysterious colors effectively represent the spirit of the work. These are most distinguished prints, not widely favored by collectors but cherished by those who know the artist and who are concerned with the artistic problems inherent in the modern school of woodblock prints. What dark experience of the soul called forth this series I do not know, but during its issue Masaji's son died, and the prints form a fitting memorial to this tragedy, although they were not originally called forth by it. Connoisseurs of the exquisite in art should know these prints, for they are some of the most expert ever issued in Japan, veritable masterpieces of printing and color. They exhibit no quick allure and one comes to them quietly after having known other prints that on the surface are much more enticing; but when one has discovered their quiet mastery one recognizes in them a milestone in contemporary Japanese woodblocks.

It is fitting, and I suppose inevitable, that Masaji's fourth clearly defined type of print should be one like the present. It has the subdued color harmony of the first type, the exquisite control of design that marked the second, and the mysterious lines and color harmonies of the third, all blended to produce a simplicity that is compelling. This is by a large margin the most sophisticated and cerebral of the prints shown in this book.

I suppose the reader has remarked that the four stages of Masaji's development parallel the four similar stages of Azechi's growth. Certainly each artist visibly grows toward a more simplified structure and a more intellectual summary of his world, but there is one conspicuous difference between the artistic experience of the two men. Azechi, born in 1902, was required by circumstance to serve his apprenticeship in the representational school of art, and it was inescapable that his first prints would be of that type. It was not until his fourth stage, reached when he was in his fifties, that he freed himself of the confinement of representation and acquired that nonobjective style which summarizes the essence of experience without lingering over its outward forms. Masaji, on the other hand, was born late enough, in 1917, to have escaped an obligatory apprenticeship in representational art—although, of course, his schooling comprised such matters—so that none of his four distinctive styles involved representational subject matter. This was also true of Iwami Reika and Maki Haku, whose work concludes this volume.

Of much greater importance, however, is the fact that in the present print Masaji reaches far beyond any petty consideration of either representation or abstraction to present the viewer with one of the most succinct summaries of what is Japanese in art that he will ever encounter. This print, which earlier I correctly placed among those whose subject matter betrayed no Japanese origin, is in spirit the most Japanese of them all. Compare it, for example, with the delightful Maekawa, which shows an obviously Japanese young lady with a lantern. The Maekawa is ostentatiously Oriental in derivation, and Western tourists who want to take home "something typically Japanese" ought to be happy to have such a subject available. (It is also, as we have seen, a lovely little thing in its own right, and no amount of facile tourist acceptance will ever spoil that.) But if one sought the essential Japanese statement on art, I think he would come much closer to "something typically Japanese" by choosing this Masaji.

Here is what I see in this rare print. On the spiritual level it is a subdued poem in praise of living a controlled and contemplative life, close to the earth. The equanimity of spirit that we seek, if we are wise, is extolled, and nature is presented to us in its subtlest mood, so as to harmonize with our own. It is an organized world, with its rocks and earth and mottled sky and restful colors well under control. It is a world of contemplation and solitude, one that Japanese intellectuals and mystics have constantly sought. It is, to be brief, a world of Zen.

On the physical level this is no ordinary print. In some curious manner, surely intended by the artist, this work conjures up visions of the Ryoan-ji garden in Kyoto, that remarkable construction which uses rippling sand and protruding rock to represent the mystery of Japan's islands rising from the sea. It is the most famous garden in Japan, a perfect evocation of an art form and one to which millions of visitors have paid homage. It is something very special, very Japanese: a small oblong of sand and rock and a little moss, but if one fails to comprehend it on first sight he can never hope to comprehend Japan. This print, with its dark rock at the bottom, its expanse of earth, its troubled sky, is surely an evocation of Ryoan-ji, the perfect representation of all that is finest in the Japanese reaction to nature.

The reader by now will have discovered that this print is simply a restatement in different terms of the first print in this book. In the earlier print Hiratsuka skillfully combined actual pictures of some of the emotional symbols that signify Japan. Obviously, he relied upon representational art. Here Masaji has utilized almost the same symbols to achieve an identical end—the significance of the Japanese earth—but he has forsworn actual representation and relied upon suggestion. And as so often occurs in art, it is probably the abstract work that ties us most securely to the real world. There may be some who will prefer, as their summary statement of Japan, Hiratsuka's admirable realism; but I suspect that upon reflection and acquaintance many will grow to understand that it was really Masaji who expressed the significance of this beautiful land.

49

YOSHIDA MASAJI: *Born March 5, 1917, in Wakayama Prefecture; now lives in Tokyo. Studied at the Kawabata Art School and, both before and after the war, in the oil-painting section of the Tokyo School of Fine Arts. Military service in China for four years, reaching the rank of lieutenant. High-school teacher of arts and crafts. Interested in sports, particularly swimming, track, and baseball.*

THE PRINT: *Artist's title: "Tsuchi 3" (Earth No. 3) or "Ground No. 3." Four plywood blocks of basswood and lauan. Printed on hosho paper but, because of an unusually large number of unsatisfactory cast-offs, the paper was exhausted and a few prints (numbers 71, 75, 76, 90, 144, 146, 182, 194, and 262) were printed on torinoko. Seven colors (sumi ink, Japanese pigments, and transparent water colors), in various mixtures, applied in the following stages: entire area excepting pink strip and small brick-red block impressed twice with greenish color; entire area except brick-red block impressed twice very lightly with pinkish brown; black area and brick-red block impressed twice each. The background texture, which varies from print to print, was obtained by applying the colors on very damp, unsized paper, producing a blotting-paper effect and causing the colors to run and blur and blend more or less haphazardly. Thin sizing of* dosa *applied to the finished print.*

THE ARTIST'S COMMENT: *"This is one of my favorites among the prints I have made. In it I attempted to capture a new sense of the beauty of space and of the materials used. I tried to combine the sense of a boundless expanse of earth, a quietly pulsating expanse of earth, with a new spatial composition."*

OX

by MAKI HAKU

THE first print in this series was a black-and-white work which illustrated the manner in which one of Japan's oldest artistic traditions could still be used to create fine contemporary work, and the starkness of black on white, produced in the old manner, was found to be pleasing to the eye and evocative to the memory. The subject matter of that first print was as traditional as one could find; the whole passage might have been lifted from one of Moronobu's early books of landscapes; and the print well demonstrated the manner in which the old could be utilized to enhance the new.

It is fitting, therefore, to conclude this cycle of prints with a second black-and-white, but one entirely different from the first. This calligraphic design by Maki is for several reasons an appropriate capstone to this book. For one thing, it demonstrates rather clearly the manner in which the younger artists are adapting the oldest techniques to their particular needs. Compare Maki's use of black with Hiratsuka's, and you will find that the younger man gains much force by utilizing three different qualities of black: the traditional solid black in the upright stroke; a medium-force black in the lower horizontal stroke; and a handsomely mottled semi-gray black in the upper curved stroke. This wide contrast yields a most pleasing effect, and the eye is constantly lured from one of the variations to the other.

A second deviation from old patterns is Maki's skillful use of three different textures of wood: the traditional solid, unblemished printing of the upright; the striking vertical graining of the lower horizontal; and the pleasing delicate mottling of the upper curve. Again, these textures carry the eye from one part of the design to the next, and when the variation in texture is wedded to the basic variation in the value of the black, a constant movement of symbol is attained, a kind of stately minuet of black and texture as first one shape and then the next takes command of the eye. Study the print for some minutes and watch this persuasive dance begin.

The third innovation is, of course, the most important. This concerns Maki's skilled use of the calligraphic symbol as the subject matter of art. In the contest several artists submitted prints constructed from calligraphic designs: some were marvelous free-flowing constructions in which the ideographs which Japan originally borrowed from China stood out conspicuously; others were bold utilizations of ideographic elements but without quite forming specific ideographs that could be identified; still others were abstractions which contained the merest suggestion of a calligraphic base.

The choice among these exciting prints finally narrowed to three: the present print; an alternate print by Maki but one stressing a conspicuous circle; and a powerful, rugged work printed with maximum boldness and a fine attention to texture by Seo Matsunoshin. The decision was finally made in favor of the present Maki for these reasons: the Seo was felt to depend too markedly upon the calligraphic structure of its symbols; the alternate Maki—a positively dazzling print—was eliminated because the circle was so obtrusive and so clearly outside the calligraphic content as to detract from the impact of the whole; the present Maki was selected without reservation because its symbol was clearly derived from calligraphy yet so subtly modified as to free it from an obvious bondage. Furthermore, the symbol was used in such a controlled manner, both in coloring-texture and in disposition, as to remind the viewer that this was a work of conscious art. As the viewer becomes familiar with this print he will grow to applaud the judges' decision.

I would have been disappointed if the contest had produced no print derived from calligraphy, for here the Oriental artist enjoys a real advantage over his Western competitor, and it is interesting to observe the attention which this branch of art is receiving in Japan today. Painters have arisen who base their entire output on calligraphic derivations and even formal calligraphers are doing an increased business. Some of the finest screens being made in the world are those consisting of six or eight stark white panels down which are splashed huge calligraphic derivations; real words are often not reproduced but an effect is given of human conversation; there is a suggestion of human thought. One of the most interesting modern phenomena is the vogue enjoyed by the free-style calligrapher who, with his inkstones and brushes and jet-black ink, creates unassociated forms that tantalize the eye with near meanings and beautiful constructions.

It is possible that this renewed interest in calligraphy comes at a time when the art is doomed, for many Japanese are reaching the conclusion that their nation can no longer bear the intolerable burden imposed by the historical accident whereby it was the Chinese ideograph that was borrowed for the writing of Japanese. Without going into all the resulting complexities here, let me only quote the wasteful experience of one Japanese scholar: "Until the age of twenty-five I spent much of my time memorizing ideographs to lay the groundwork for scholarship. At one time I must have known about eighteen thousand, and what the Westerner doesn't understand is that it was just as difficult to memorize number 18,001 as it had been to master number 101. What's more painful, today I've forgotten all but about eight thousand. My years were wasted on a futile system."

There is much discussion of remedies. Some critics advocate abandoning ideographs altogether and substituting one or the other of the syllabaries that the Japanese developed to use in conjunction with the ideographs. Others propose cutting the number of ideographs back to the less than two thousand now used by newspapers. Radicals argue: "Don't try to patch up the system. Abandon ideographs and local syllabaries in one sweep and use the international roman alphabet, like other civilized nations." In this latter system, *romaji,* the Japanese word for, say, tree would no longer be represented by the ideograph 木 but by the romanized spelling of its actual pronunciation, *ki.*

But whenever critics propose abandonment of the ideographs, those traditionalists who love the intellectual history of Japan experience a surge of nostalgia for the cumbersome, time-crowned pictures of words, and innovation is defeated. No Westerner can appreciate the emotional value that attaches to the handsome ideographs with which the Oriental grows up. In our Western system the cold and casual arrangement of an alphabet that produces the word man bears no emotional freight with it, but in the Oriental system the ideograph that represents the word man, 人, is an actual artistic picture of the concept man. Thus the Japanese boy destined to be an artist is constantly surrounded by a world of vivid and vital pictures. He memorizes them as the avenue to thought; he learns to reproduce them in an artistic manner, for to copy them inartistically would be to proclaim oneself a fool; and throughout his life these handsome symbols affect him in a manner not known in countries that use the more impersonal alphabet.

I suppose it would be logical to describe the recent resurgence of calligraphy in art as a form of chauvinism, an automatic protest against change; but we do not need to seek too cleverly for the *raison d'être* of a work like this Maki print. Possibly a return to calligraphic symbols would have taken place even though the language system were not under review. The original ideographs were themselves authentic works of art—simplified, forceful, evocative—and the symbols derived from them are artistic messengers of the most exalted power. They conjure up recollections of children's stories told long ago, of battles in which the nation was forged, of the poetic flight of the human imagination, and of the hard, grinding daily pursuit of man's livelihood. As such they are symbols of a power unknown in the Western world.

Japan's new calligraphic art, therefore, derives from one of the oldest traditions in Asia and one of the most powerful. To the Westerner it must remain a recondite art, perhaps the more compelling for that very reason.

53

MAKI HAKU: *Born September 27, 1924, in Ibaragi Prefecture, near Tokyo, where he still lives. Graduated from Ibaragi Teachers' College and is now vice-principal of an elementary school. Studied for two years under Onchi Koshiro with the Modern Print Study Group. Other interests include carving seals and writing poetry.*

THE PRINT: *Artist's title: "Ushi" (Ox). Four blocks (cherry, lauan, and sen) of both solid board and plywood. One block printed in gaufrage to define the outer limits of the print with its embossed line, and the others printed in sumi ink and black Japanese-style pigment, on natural-color kozo paper. One impression for the gaufrage block and two impressions each for the black blocks.*

THE ARTIST'S COMMENT (*freely translated*): *"This print is based upon the character* 牛, *meaning cow or ox. I have here tried to give our cultural heritage of such ideographs a modern feel, but in an Oriental style. This meant trying to capture the typically Japanese expression of the beauty of space, the sense of reverence for and persistent pursuit of boundless space, while at the same time taking advantage of the boundary provided by the beauty and life of the paper itself. The beauty of sumi, in its monochrome black, penetrates to the back of the paper and forbids decorative exaggeration or irrelevancies. This effect combines with a succinct and straightforward approach to create a space and an expression that, though intentionally compact, still have a quiet and gentle spread. The two small red seals are an integral part of the composition, providing color and a focal point and thus making the impersonality of the sumi's space deeper and wider and warmer."*

IN CONCLUSION

HOW were the foregoing ten prints chosen? In order to insure obtaining a selection that would epitomize the best work being done today by the print artists of Japan, on October 1, 1959, a contest was announced under the sponsorship of the publisher and myself. Among the terms of the contest the following may be of interest: Ten cash prizes of $1,278 each. Contest open to any artist closely identified with the contemporary Japanese print movement. Not more than three prints by any one artist. Each entry to be an original, unpublished print of the designated size, self-designed, self-carved, and self-printed, with no restrictions on subject matter, style, or technique. For use in this book, each prize-winning artist to supply 510 numbered copies of his winning print, printed either by himself or by an artisan under his supervision, striking off not more than ten additional copies for his own files, and then to destroy the blocks. It was also announced that the best hundred or so prints would be shown in exhibitions to be held at Takashimaya Department Store in Tokyo under the auspices of the three leading Japanese associations of print artists and at Asia House in New York under the auspices of the Japan Society of New York.

As a result of the wide broadcast of this invitation, 120 artists submitted a total of 275 prints for judging, and all but a very few of the greatest names in the movement were represented. These prints then went to two panels of judges, one in Tokyo and the other in New York. The judges were:

Carl Zigrosser, Director of the Department of Prints, Philadelphia Museum of Art, author of numerous books on fine prints, and a distinguished art scholar.

Oliver Statler, author of *Modern Japanese Prints: An Art Reborn* and *Japanese Inn*, owner of one of the most extensive collections of modern Japanese prints, and the leading expert in the field.

Elise Grilli, famous and delightful art critic for Tokyo's leading English-language newspaper, the *Japan Times*, and author of more critical essays on contemporary Japanese artists than any other Western writer. She has a wide knowledge of Japanese cultural activity and an enviable manner of expressing forthright opinions.

Nathan Polowetzky, then in the Tokyo Bureau of the Associated Press, owner of an extensive collection of *avant-garde* European and Japanese art. An excited amateur in the best sense of the word, Mr. Polowetzky has proved himself to be a staunch friend of artists and a sensitive judge of their work.

Dr. Zigrosser and Mr. Statler did their judging in New York; Mrs. Grilli and Mr. Polowestzky did theirs at the same time in Tokyo. As can be deduced from the results, the two panels did not consult with each other, nor did they know each other's decisions until the judging had been completed. The heart of the instructions under which each panel operated was: "Please nominate up to twelve entries which, offered as a group, will best represent the richness and power of the modern Japanese print. An almost perfect guiding principle would be this question: Which prints, varied in technique, style, texture, coloring, and content, would I myself like to own?"

In their nominations the New York judges tended slightly toward the historical and representational, recommending a strong list of prints that recapitulated the experience of the art from its early-1900 days down to the present. Hiratsuka, Maekawa, Azechi, Sekino, and Kitaoka were chosen as representative of the admirable men who had developed this art and kept it alive during difficult days. The Tokyo judges, on the other hand, evidently felt that the grand figures of the past had long ago received their just encomiums, and they concentrated their nominations on the more recent arrivals and the most vital of the nonrepresentational work. None of the five famous artists chosen in New York appeared on the Tokyo list.

After this first stage in the judging, each judge was then asked individually to list in order of preference all the prints nominated by either panel. With these ratings before them, the Tuttle editors, to whom fell the responsibility of deciding which ten of the nominations would together produce the handsomest, most meaningful book, then began the difficult task of making the final selections.

If the editors had accepted only the New York choices, the result would have been a distinguished group of prints rather heavy on the traditional side but a group that would have well illustrated the principal currents in the world of contemporary prints since about 1900. On the other hand, had the editors been guided solely by the Tokyo judges, the result would have been a dazzling, radical portrait of the most venturesome efforts of today. The reader might have gained the impression that the school had started about six years ago in the full international style, and he would have caught only vague intimations of what had gone before in the earlier years of this century. It is interesting that not one of the Tokyo nominations betrayed in its content any suggestion of Japanese subject matter, unless abstract calligraphic symbols should be so defined.

Obviously, there was little duplication between the two lists, but where it did occur it was significant. Both pairs of judges selected prints by Watanabe, Iwami, and Maki. Thus there was general agreement that these three strong artists should be represented, and this wish was respected by the editors.

In selecting the next few prints, the editors decided that, since the public for whom the book was intended might not be as familiar with the earlier work as were the Tokyo judges, the considerations which guided the New York panel should be given preference. This automatically meant the inclusion of Hiratsuka, Maekawa, and Azechi, a judgment with which I certainly could not argue since they had all submitted fine prints and were among my dearest friends in Japan, their work having been among the very first I had acquired when I started collecting in the field.

On the other hand, this early decision meant that three of the vibrant Tokyo nominations of modern work would have to be dropped, and I am still sorry that this had to be so, for my personal tastes incline strongly toward that style of art. Well, the artists so dropped are young men and perhaps at some later date we can do justice to them. In the meantime old Maekawa has died, and I am grateful that he lived long enough to receive his prize.

Thus six prints had been chosen, leaving but four vacancies. The editors, consulting both their own tastes and the judges' ratings, concluded that it would be ridiculous to omit the Shima "Birds," and it was included without further discussion. The Kinoshita "Faces" was also practically automatic, since everyone was attracted to it. Yoshida Masaji's "Earth" was selected as most representative of the kind of print the Tokyo judges liked best, and I cannot imagine a happier choice. As I have intimated in my remarks on this print, it has become for me the highlight of the collection, and I am pleased to note that it was also Mrs. Grilli's first choice.

I was responsible for the selection of only one print, Mori's "Comic Shinto Dancers," and thereby hangs an explanation. This print gained from all the judges a respectable rating, but never at the top. When the judges' nominations were sent to me in Mexico, where I was working at the time, I immediately liked this print and was somewhat disappointed that it had not been rated higher. I let the matter rest until I found that each Mexican artist who came to see the prints chose this as his favorite. They said: "Such wonderful Indian force!" "Such a universal sense of comedy!" One man said firmly: "Even if you have to throw the others away, keep that one. It is the work of art."

Since I was not writing a book about Mexican art I disregarded the opinions of these artists and did not report them to the editors; but after I had returned home I found that all my Pennsylvania friends who were associated with the arts were reacting in the same way to this print. They said: "This is the one that speaks across the room." "This is the theatrical work that summarizes what we are all after." When I heard half a dozen such comments I decided that my initial judgment had been correct and that this was indeed a fine print. I thereupon asked the editors to include it.

Thus, in one way or another, the ten prints were chosen by a group of Americans who respect and treasure the work being done in Japan today. I am convinced that a typical group of prints has resulted and that study of them will inform the reader of what is happening in Japan today.

In concluding, it is only appropriate, I think, to list the prints that were nominated by either panel of judges but for which space could not be found in this book. I do this for a special reason: the blocks from which the prints included here were printed have been destroyed and no further copies can ever be offered for sale. Those that were nominated but not included are still available in Japan and can be purchased for reasonable cost. They would do justice to any collection:

NOMINATED BY THE TOKYO JUDGES

AMANO KAZUMI: "Resting Bird." A large rooster in roughly carved black and white.

FUKAMIZU SHOSAKU: "Autumn Rain." A delicate etching showing a human face against a rainy windowpane, done in black and white.

HAGIWARA HIDEO: "Stone." A somber, beautifully printed abstraction in dark iridescent coloring.

IKEDA SHUZO: "Fisherman." A tall, angular fisherman in strong black and white.

ISOBE YUKIHISA: "Composition." An impression of a crow in a storm, composed of swirling splashes of black.

KIDOKORO YOSHIMI: "Wind." A beautifully controlled composition printed in a variety of subdued colors.

SEO MATSUNOSHIN: Untitled. The calligraphic design in black and white described on page 52.

YOSHIDA HODAKA: "Guardian Deity of Roads." A brilliantly colored abstraction.

NOMINATED BY THE NEW YORK JUDGES

IWAMI REIKA: "Winter Composition 1." An abstraction with bold dark areas, sparse colors, and a wintry glitter of rime, similar to the print included in this book.

KITAOKA FUMIO: "Autumn." One of the most colorful prints in the competition.

MAKI HAKU: Untitled. Another striking black-and-white calligraphic shape that forms a handsome pair with the Maki abstraction presented in this book.

SEKINO JUN'ICHIRO: "Prayer." A most effective Negro head, with hands clasped, against a background of Japanese newspaper carrying a related story.

TAKAHASHI SHIN'ICHI: "Street Corner." An exciting, vividly colored abstraction.

WATANABE SADAO: Untitled. Biblically inspired as many of this artist's works are, the spiritual intention of this print is rendered in the same hardy dye-technique of the prize-winner included in this book.